3 00 W9-BNY-271

Main   June 2016

Damaged bottom, noted
12/20/16 -SSP

Being Me (and Loving It)

This item no longer
belongs to Davenport
Public Library

of related interest

The Big Book of EVEN MORE Therapeutic Activity Ideas for Children and Teens
Inspiring Arts-Based Activities and Character Education Curricula
Lindsey Joiner
ISBN 978 1 84905 749 3
eISBN 978 1 78450 196 9

Believing You Can is the First Step to Achieving
A CBT and Attribution Programme to Improve
Self-Belief in Students aged 8–12
Alicia R. Chodkiewicz and Christopher Boyle
ISBN 978 1 84905 625 0
eISBN 978 1 78450 098 6

The KidsKope Peer Mentoring Programme
A Therapeutic Approach to Help Children and
Young People Build Resilience and Deal with Conflict
Nina Wroe and Penny McFarlane
ISBN 978 1 84905 500 0
eISBN 978 0 85700 903 6

Helping Children to Build Self-Esteem
A Photocopiable Activities Book
Second Edition
Deborah M. Plummer
ISBN 978 1 84310 488 9
eISBN 978 1 84642 609 4

Life Coaching for Kids
A Practical Manual to Coach Children and
Young People to Success, Well-being and Fulfilment
Nikki Giant
ISBN 978 1 84905 982 4
eISBN 978 0 85700 884 8

DAVENPORT PUBLIC LIBRARY
321 MAIN STREET
DAVENPORT, IOWA 52801-1490

Being Me (and Loving It)

Stories and activities to help build self-esteem, confidence, body image and resilience in children

Naomi Richards and Julia Hague

Jessica Kingsley *Publishers*
London and Philadelphia

First published in 2016
by Jessica Kingsley Publishers
73 Collier Street
London N1 9BE, UK
and
400 Market Street, Suite 400
Philadelphia, PA 19106, USA

www.jkp.com

Copyright © Naomi Richards and Julia Hague 2016

All rights reserved. No part of this publication may be reproduced in any material form (including photocopying of any pages other than those marked with a ★, storing it in any medium by electronic means and whether or not transiently or incidentally to some other use of this publication) without the written permission of the copyright owner except in accordance with the provisions of the Copyright, Designs and Patents Act 1988 or under the terms of a licence issued by the Copyright Licensing Agency Ltd, Saffron House, 6–10 Kirby Street, London EC1N 8TS. Applications for the copyright owner's written permission to reproduce any part of this publication should be addressed to the publisher.

Warning: The doing of an unauthorised act in relation to a copyright work may result in both a civil claim for damages and criminal prosecution.

All pages marked ★ may be photocopied for personal use with this programme, but may not be reproduced for any other purposes without the permission of the publisher.

Library of Congress Cataloging in Publication Data
A CIP catalog record for this book is available from the Library of Congress

British Library Cataloguing in Publication Data
A CIP catalogue record for this book is available from the British Library

ISBN 978 1 84905 713 4
eISBN 978 1 78450 236 2

Printed and bound in the United States

This book is for all children. Its aim is to help them to understand the wonderful but often painful side of growing up, to learn how to manage any problems they come up against and to enjoy their primary years. Most of all, it will help them to accept and love who they are and, in doing so, see everyone around them as equal.

ACKNOWLEDGEMENTS

This book would not have been possible without chance meetings. Every part of its journey to reach your hands has unfolded at the right place at the right time. Coming together and sharing our passion for helping children to cope with the challenges they face as they grow up has been a delight for us both. Thank you to both of our families and close friends for supporting us and giving us space to write it and for E and K for adding their thoughts too. Thank you to the whole editorial team at Jessica Kingsley Publishers and to their marketing team for getting it out there. It is great that you see and share our vision to make a difference in young children's lives.

CONTENTS

PART 3: SELF-ESTEEM AND SELF-WORTH

PART 4: PEER PRESSURE

PART 5: BEING UNIQUE

PART 8: FITTING IN

ABOUT THE AUTHORS

NAOMI RICHARDS

Naomi is known as The Kids Coach, a life coach who provides coaching for children on issues such as self-esteem, confidence building, social interaction, challenging negative thoughts and beliefs, friendships and school problems.

She empowers children to solve problems for themselves and passes on valuable skills that they will need for life. She does this through interactive and supportive coaching sessions and shows them there is more than one way to solve a problem. Some solutions are common sense and practical but many are innovative, creative and original. A subtle change to the way a child thinks or does can have a huge impact on their life.

Naomi was the first life coach for children in the UK and has been coaching since 2004. As well as coaching internationally she runs tailor-made workshops for children in schools, writes about the world of children and parenting in the press, is a motivational speaker for children and the author of *The Parent's Toolkit* published by Random House in 2012.

Naomi has been recognized as a Remarkable Woman – a female entrepreneur who is leading the way in a chosen career path – an initiative backed by Nokia, and in 2013 entered into the realm of conferences for girls aged 11–13 years. In 2015 she launched a range of products to help boost children's self-esteem.

JULIA HAGUE

Julia has a wealth of experience in the environment of primary and secondary education given her 16 years of working within the administration of a private girls' school in London.

A writer from a young age and a mother of a grown-up daughter herself, Julia's passion is in showing parents and educators how they can instil a healthy self-esteem and body image in children from an early age and help them to understand friendship issues and bullying from the very start.

Julia uses her unique storytelling style to show children, from the perspective of others just like them, how their feelings on subjects such as friendship and relationships with others are quite normal, and in doing so provides the children themselves with the tools and confidence to cope with friendship issues and peer pressure, including bullying, while they move through their education and beyond.

Having been born in and lived in London all her life, Julia has recently moved to Cornwall with her husband and is enjoying a new life in the country. In her spare time, Julia heads up her own event company, which has successfully specialized in charity fundraising in the world of science fiction TV for the past ten years.

INTRODUCTION FOR EDUCATORS

This book has primarily been created to be used as part of Personal, Social and Health Education (PSHE) with groups of children or in one-to-one settings. It can also be used by parents with their children. It is a unique educational teaching resource, as its structure is around real-life stories that all have key messages within them. Reading the stories out to a group of children or with an individual and working through the accompanying activities will give children a deeper understanding of who they are and how to solve problems. Problem-solving is not a natural skill for all children and therefore it needs to be taught. The main purpose of the book is self-esteem based but it also addresses friendships, peer pressure, body image, social media and puberty.

It can be hard growing up in the 21st century for many children as there are a great deal of external influences and challenges around today that they have to deal with. There is the pressure to look and act a certain way and both are having a detrimental effect on children's self-esteem. This low self-esteem is affecting children's relationships and their energy for life as the way they think and feel about themselves is so negative. They struggle to accept who they are and how they look. Most of this negativity stems from the way their peer groups are interacting with them and what they are seeing in the media in terms of what their role models look like, are doing and are saying. Understandably, these role models tend to be those who are on TV – in reality shows, on both UK and American soaps, and pop stars. Many parents would rather their children did not aspire to be or behave like these people.

All children need to have a healthy self-esteem so that they are able to cope with difficult situations and be resilient. School life and socializing in extracurricular group activities can be hard, and not everyone is nice. Children can be quite mean to each other so we need to prepare them for the different personality types they are going to come across.

In terms of the friendships between children and the emotions that go with tricky friendship situations, this book will help children understand the situation and challenge the negative thoughts and feelings they encounter. The book will also help to equip children with valuable life skills such as seeing things from another person's point of view and decision making.

In the book, the children will hear stories from boys and girls the same age as them, with similar experiences, which should make them feel 'they are just like me'. We hope that they will see that beauty comes in lots of different guises, that personality is pretty much everything, that friendships are not always straightforward, that situations don't have to stay the same and that children need to appreciate and accept who they are.

There are 29 stories in total for educators to pick and choose from. They are all powerful and inspiring and easy to listen to and understand. Each story has an introduction that can be read out loud to a group (such as a whole class), smaller groups or an individual. If reading to an individual the language needs to change to focus on that one child. There is an exercise the children can do before reading the story and there are discussion questions to use after the story, along with a selection of activities that take into account the age of the children and their knowledge. They are all for Key Stage 1–2 year groups. An educator can choose how in-depth those discussions are and they can be adjusted to the age of the child. There are discussion notes to go with the questions that can be used if educators want to go into more detail on that subject area.

The activities have been developed with different learning styles in mind.

Part 1

BODY IMAGE

STORY ONE

STICKIE OUT TUMMY

(ABOUT HOW STICKING OUT TUMMIES ARE NORMAL)

TALIA'S STORY

EDUCATORS' NOTES

Suggested age for story – 5–6 years old

When children change for PE at this age they notice the shape of other children's bodies with a focus on tummies. They see that some children have a more rounded tummy and some children do not have a tummy at all. Children need to realize that they are growing and that they will put on a bit of weight before they grow in height. We need to teach children this so they can be more relaxed about changing in front of others and feel happier about what they look like while they are growing. If they accept what is happening to their bodies then they will be happier and feel confident at school, at home and with friendships.

All pre- and post-lesson exercises can be used for evaluation purposes if required.

LEARNING OUTCOMES

- Each child's tummy and body is different.
- Tummies do stick out when children are growing.
- We should not be embarrassed about how we look.
- Children need to love their bodies.

INTRODUCTION STATEMENT

Today we are going to talk about bodies and how they grow. We all have parts of our body that we like and there are some bits we don't like as much. Some of you may not have thought much about your tummy and its shape, and others of you might have, but tummies have an important role. Our tummies have a great purpose in that they help keep our trousers and our skirts up and they also protect all the things that are inside it. Everyone's tummy is different – some are round, some long and some short just like the rest of how we look. Some children have an outie for a belly button and others have an innie. Both are normal.

Tummies change as we get older, like the rest of us, so we should love our tummies now because they may not be the same bouncy, soft tummy forever.

PRE- AND POST-LESSON EXERCISE

Ask the children to write down one thing they like about their tummy and what they think it is there for. After reading the story ask them to write down what they have learnt about tummies to see how their thoughts have changed.

I am going to read you Talia's story. Talia noticed that although her tummy was different to her friends it was a part of her and she should love it.

TALIA'S STORY

I think that having a sticking out tummy is the best thing in the world.

My friend Lexi says that my tummy is like a little cushion.

Sometimes, when we're playing together, she puts her head on it and puts her arms around me and squeezes me tight. Lexi loves my tummy.

I didn't always know I had a sticking out tummy.

But one day, when I was four, my mummy's friend Auntie Lisa came to tea and brought her daughter Susie with her. Susie has a sticking out tummy too but I had never noticed before. She ran over to me and pointed her finger and hugged me.

I asked her what she was pointing at.

Susie started giggling and pulled her t-shirt up and rubbed her tummy.

'You got a stickie out tummy just like me. Mummy says stickie out tummies are great. It's soft and squishy and I like it.'

Susie giggled again and ran off towards my toy box.

I pulled my t-shirt up and looked at my tummy. I noticed it was a tiny bit bigger than the rest of me. Sticking out. So I poked it. It was very soft.

After Susie had gone home that day I asked my mummy why I had a stickie out tummy.

Mummy pulled me onto her lap and gave me a huge cuddle and kissed my cheek.

'When you're growing up your tummy grows a bit faster than the rest of you and so it sticks out a bit. Lots of little girls and boys have sticking out tummies as they grow up. And when you're a lot older your tummy might go flat. But you might have a stickie out tummy forever and that's okay because it's part of you.'

The next day I ran into school and couldn't wait to talk to Lexi about my discovery. Lexi poked it and giggled. She poked hers and frowned.

'I haven't got one,' she said.

'My mummy says flat tummies are great too,' I told her, and hugged her. 'I love your tummy too, Lexi.'

Copyright © Naomi Richards and Julia Hague 2016

Actually none of the girls or boys in my class ever said anything about my stickie out tummy at school.

But now I knew I had one because Susie had pointed it out. I noticed a few of my friends had sticking out tummies too.

And I found someone else who has a stickie out tummy and I love her so much too.

My dog Bella is beautiful and she loves cuddling with me on the sofa when I'm watching TV. Straight after Susie had pointed out my tummy, I noticed Bella had one too. It was soft and squishy and when we cuddled up together she would lie on my tummy and I could feel her soft stickie out tummy against mine.

So my mummy was right. Stickie out tummies are really okay. I like mine. Susie likes hers. But flat tummies are also okay. Lexi loves hers. Secretly I'd like my tummy to stay sticking out. But if it doesn't that's okay.

I'm kind of happy that Susie pointed mine out to me.

Actually I'm very happy.

Copyright © Naomi Richards and Julia Hague 2016

NOTES TO SUPPORT THE DISCUSSION

We all grow up at different speeds. As you get older you grow out and then grow up. It can make you feel sad when you grow out and then have to wait to grow taller. Just remember this is how we all get to being a grown-up and that the same thing happens to everyone. Sometimes your tummy may be soft and round and sometimes a little smaller. It is all part of the growing up process.

If you feel like you are the only one with a stickie out tummy tell Mum or Dad how you feel as I am sure they can show you old photos of when they were a child and you will see they were just the same.

DISCUSSION QUESTIONS TO ASK THE CHILDREN

- What do you think about Talia's story?

- Do you have a stickie out tummy too?

- What's the best thing about a stickie out tummy?

- Would you want your tummy to be different?

- What other parts of your body do you really love?

ACTIVITIES TO DO WITH THE CHILDREN

HELPING A FRIEND WHO DOES NOT LIKE THEIR TUMMY

Ask the children, 'What can we do when a friend says they have a sticking out tummy and they don't like it?' Get them to shout out answers and then ask them to role play them out. One person says they have a sticking out tummy and the other tells them not to worry and shares what they learnt from the story.

HELPING CHILDREN TO HAVE POSITIVE THOUGHTS ABOUT THEIR BODY

Get each child to draw a picture of themselves and then write in their favourite parts of their body and why they like them.

GET POETIC

Ask the children to write a poem about tummies and how wonderful they are. It does not have to rhyme.

HOW MANY?

Ask the children to make a list of five things that are round and what is so great about their shape. For example, a ball. Get them to share their list with the group.

A SHORT STORY

(ABOUT BEING SHORT)

ANGEL'S STORY

EDUCATORS' NOTES

Suggested age for story – 8–10 years old

Children need to be aware that we all grow at different speeds and that our height is determined by how tall our parents and grandparents are. Some children will end up smaller than others and there is nothing they can do about it but accept who they are. We cannot control the speed at which we grow and so children need to understand that they have growth spurts at different times.

Tall and small mean different things to different people and both have benefits. The children will realize what these benefits are from the story and learn to accept the height they and their friends are. Self-acceptance will build self-confidence and self-esteem.

All pre- and post-lesson exercises can be used for evaluation purposes if required.

LEARNING OUTCOMES

- There are benefits of being smaller than your peers.

- Every person develops at a different rate.

- As adults we can end up being the same height as our peers.

- Take advantage of whatever height you are rather than wanting to be different.

INTRODUCTION STATEMENT

Today's session is all about how we look – in fact how tall we are. We need to be sensitive to other people's height, as they might not like being smaller than their friends and get upset about it. There is a famous saying that 'good things come in small packages'. It is not entirely true as good things come in all different shapes and sizes. There are wonderful advantages of being smaller than other people and if you are smaller than your friends right now you need to realize what these advantages are. You can fit into small hiding places when playing hide and seek, possibly run faster than your friends as you are closer to the ground – this is good when playing rugby and you will never get told to duck down in the cinema. The story we are going to read will help you see that there is nothing wrong with being smaller than your friends and that you are who and what you are. You may feel you are small now but you will not be forever. You will not be the same height as you are now, I assure you.

PRE- AND POST-LESSON EXERCISE

Ask the children to write down what they think about their height before reading the story. What do they think about a person's height? At the end of the lesson ask them if their thoughts have changed about themselves or about how they feel about others who are smaller than them. What changed?

Here is Angel's story. She learnt to appreciate her height despite not being the same size as her friends.

ANGEL'S STORY

My dad calls me Shortcake.

He means it in a nice way.

Usually when I've had a terrible day at school or I'm just walking past him, he'll ruffle my hair and smile at me when he says it.

He says being short, which I am, and being sweet (which he says I am) is the best of everything – just like a shortcake biscuit. Yeah, I know it's kind of cute. But he forgets that by saying it he just keeps on reminding me…about being short.

Maybe I'll always be short. Mum is short. My auntie is short. My sister is short.

I don't know why, but I always wanted to be tall. I think because all the models on TV and all my favourite actresses are tall.

But we're all different. I know that. I've seen actresses on TV who are short, they're just not my favourites. But they are popular.

My dad asked me once why I always compare myself to people on TV or in magazines. I didn't know what to say. I don't know who else to compare myself to.

My friends I guess.

But I don't look at them and think I wish I could be like her because… well…they're my friends. I just like them. Doesn't matter if they're small or big, short or tall. I don't want to be the same as them. I don't even think about it.

Then I think if I'm not comparing myself to them, they're probably not comparing themselves to me and so my height is okay. It's not obvious to them, I think, that I am short.

Then the next day I see a TV show and want to be tall again.

I am much better than I used to be, mind you.

I used to think that if I was tall my life would be perfect. I'd look good in all the latest fashions, walk like the models do on the catwalks and be perfect. And if I looked perfect my life would be perfect. What was I thinking?

If I was tall, I'd still have the same life, the same school, the same house and all that would happen would be I'd be able to speak to other people's faces rather than their shoulders.

Copyright © Naomi Richards and Julia Hague 2016

I'd still look the same. Just have longer legs or a longer body.

That's it. Nothing else.

Maybe I could be a model. Sure. But maybe I don't want to be a model. I never thought of that. Being tall doesn't mean you really want or have to be a model. Or an actress.

Actually I love animals so much I'd love to be a vet when I grow up.

So I watch loads and loads of programmes about vets. There's plenty of them on TV.

And I realize that being short is kinda cool if I want to work with animals.

Being short would mean I'd be nearer to the ground to bend down to the animals.

Most animals are small. Well dogs and cats and bunnies and things.

If you're tall, you'd have to crouch down small to reach them or kneel down. That can't be comfortable!

Me? I could just bend easily or even be at the right height when they get put onto the examination table.

Cool.

And sticking your hand up a cow's bum. I saw that on one programme and the vet was really tall and had to lean at this really uncomfortable angle! I would be at eye level, so…result!

When I told my mum and dad that, they couldn't stop laughing!

Being short means that I can sometimes wear clothes that tall girls can't get into and sometimes I find clothes which are in the junior department of a shop rather than in the pre-teen section where some of my friends buy their clothes. It means I am never going to be wearing the same thing as them.

Result!

It also means that when it comes to watching films at school and cool things like that, the teacher always moves the short girls and boys to the front of the hall!

So we get the best, best view!

Result again!!

So yeah, being short doesn't have to be bad.

Being short is just…well, as Dad says…the best of everything!

Copyright © Naomi Richards and Julia Hague 2016

NOTES TO SUPPORT THE DISCUSSION

Being shorter than other people can be really advantageous. Even though sometimes you might feel left out, there's no need to. For example, just because you might not have been picked for teams like basketball, there are lots of other sports and activities you will get picked for where height does not matter or where being shorter is best. Remember that everyone is different and that we all come in different sizes. We can see that whenever we look around at other people. It's better to take advantage of whatever height you are and see the benefits rather than wish to be something you are not.

DISCUSSION QUESTIONS TO ASK THE CHILDREN

- What do you think about Angel? What did you think about her attitude?

- Do you know of a friend who finds being short a problem? If so, how?

- What advice would you give your friend if they felt sad about being smaller than their friends? What is it about being small they don't like?

- Can you think of somewhere where being small might be an advantage, like Angel's vet?

ACTIVITIES TO DO WITH THE CHILDREN

WRITING A LETTER
Ask the children to write a letter to their friend outlining all the benefits of being smaller than their friends. Make it chatty and light-hearted.

TURNING THE NEGATIVE FEELING INTO A POSITIVE ONE
Ask the children to come up with three pieces of advice they would give to a friend who said that they were called names for being small. What could they tell them to think or do differently? Ask them to write them down.

ON SCREEN
Ask each child to think of a role model they love who is on TV who is smaller than their co-stars. It can be a real person, a character in a film or a cartoon character. Get them to draw that person as best they can and next to their drawing write sentences or single words to describe what they love most about that person/ character.

GETTING POETIC

Using the letters from the word 'SHORTCAKE', get the children to write a poem about being short.

HEAD IN THE CLOUDS

(ABOUT TOWERING OVER OTHERS)

VICTORIA'S STORY

EDUCATORS' NOTES

Suggested age for story – 9–11 years old

Children need to realize that some children can be very self-conscious or sensitive about their height. This can affect their self-esteem as they don't feel they fit in. The story chosen addresses the height issue and has several points of discussion following it, along with a selection of activities that can be done with these year groups. The activities take into account the ability and understanding of the children.

All pre- and post-lesson exercises can be used for evaluation purposes if required.

LEARNING OUTCOMES

- Being tall has many advantages.
- Children grow at different rates.
- Self-acceptance.
- Understanding how others may feel about their height.

INTRODUCTION STATEMENT

We are going to talk about height today. Have a look around you. Some of your friends are taller than you and others are smaller than you. Some of you may love the height you are and some of you may feel that you are too tall and would rather be a little shorter. One thing we know for sure is that you are all still growing and those of you who are tall may not grow much more.

PRE- AND POST-LESSON EXERCISE

Ask the children to write down how they think tall people may feel about their height and the benefits of being tall before reading the story. Ask them after the story what they have learnt about being tall and get them to write it down.

I am going to share with you Victoria's story. Victoria did not like being tall as all her friends were the same height as each other and shorter than she was. She felt very self-conscious about her height as she towered over them. She did not need to feel this way. She needed to realize and appreciate that being tall has its advantages.

VICTORIA'S STORY

I saw a giraffe on TV last week.

All graceful with lovely long legs and a beautiful neck looking so content that he could reach the really high branches of the tree and eat way up there, out of everyone's reach.

He didn't care whether the elephant wandering below him thought he was too tall.

Or whether the monkeys swinging in the trees were laughing at him.

Difficult to tell really.

Monkeys sound as if they are laughing all the time.

But this giraffe just went on eating, sometimes stretching out his legs so he could reach the lower branches.

And he was sooo happy.

And get this…

I was jealous.

Not of the giraffe eating branches way up high of course. That would be silly.

I mean, I don't eat branches.

No, I was jealous that he looked so pleased with himself.

Because when I watched the TV I realized that I wasn't as happy as him. Not really.

Because I've been called everything. Beanpole. Telegraph legs. Stick insect. Probably more names than that to be honest, but those three are the ones I hear most often at school.

I'm really tall. Like, really.

There's no one in my year who gets anywhere near me. Not in my class. Not in the other class. Not even in the year above me. And that includes the boys. And what makes it even worse is that they're about to go to secondary school in a few months' time.

But I haven't always been like this. I was normal. Well, normal as far as height goes.

Nothing different. Same height as my friends in nursery. Even in reception.

Copyright © Naomi Richards and Julia Hague 2016

Then suddenly I started to grow.

My really irritating auntie said she would need to put a brick on my head if I grew any faster. Because 'girls don't grow that tall'. So she said.

Mum was really cross with her for saying that.

'Of course girls grow that tall,' she said, and I saw her give my auntie this really angry look.

It didn't upset me…because I'd heard it all before. For that past year. Since the other children realized they had to look up at me when they talked to me. That I was sometimes in their way when they were looking at the whiteboard in class.

So in the end the teacher moved me to the back. So everyone could see without straining their necks looking past me.

And clothes.

At first I think they thought it was cool that I was wearing shorter skirts.

For about a week I was on the verge of being hauled into the cool group. The group where short skirts are everything.

But then they realized that it was only because Mum couldn't keep up with me growing so fast, so Mum let the skirt hems down and within a month the skirt was short again.

So she'd have to buy another one. But Mum didn't say anything.

Nothing. She was good like that.

So I told the kids at school that it was because I was growing so fast.

You know it's the kind of thing you can tell a friend.

But tell a cool group something utterly uncool and you get the reaction I got.

So they ignored me for a while.

I think they sort of got jealous of the shorter skirt thing. Because their mums had bought them longer skirts so they could grow into them.

You know, like mums usually do.

They last longer if they start longer.

That's what Mrs Pickering used to say when some of the girls rolled their waistbands over to make them shorter and she made them unravel them. She told me to do it once and then looked surprised when I

Copyright © Naomi Richards and Julia Hague 2016

showed her the skirt was not rolled up. Then she sent a letter home to mum telling her my skirt was too short.

So that's when mum started having to buy me skirts more often.

My friend Amy said that I could be a model when I'm older, if I wanted to.

That having long legs and being tall is what every girl wants to be.

Do they? Really?

I don't think that's true.

I guess because I've already got it. The whole being tall thing. I can't imagine anyone wanting it.

However, I'm popular when the netball team gets picked. Yeah I can slam a ball pretty neatly into the net. Mostly every time. But I don't like netball and I don't want to be a professional netball player as my PE teacher keeps suggesting. She talks to my parents every time she sees them and tries to persuade them to put me in for the Junior County Club.

But Mum and Dad would never force me. So they politely tell her that if I ever say I want to do that, then I can.

But it will be my choice.

Go Mum and Dad!

I sat down on the bed the other night in front of my computer and did a kind of chart.

It was after I'd seen the giraffe.

I really liked that giraffe.

He was like my hero.

The chart had one column with all the good things about being tall and then another column with all the bad things.

I must admit that the good things column was longer than the bad things column.

But I really had to think.

This is what I came up with for the good ones:

- I can reach things down from cupboards easier.

- I rescued the cat from next door that was stuck on a branch just out of reach of Mrs Conway, who is quite short.

- I can see over people's heads at school assembly or at the cinema so no one blocks my view. Even when I'm at the back.

Copyright © Naomi Richards and Julia Hague 2016

- I can stand in deeper water than my friends at the swimming pool. Which is kinda cool.

- I can get onto the rides at the theme park, which a couple of my friends can't.

- I've been horse riding and got given a bigger horse. I love bigger horses. Much quieter than those racing ponies my friends end up with. And I could get up on him easily. Some of my friends needed mounting blocks.

- I play a mean game of netball. But I still don't want to do it for the rest of my life.

- When we were on holiday everyone wanted me to play beach volleyball. I loved that.

So what were the bad bits?

- The teasing. And the jealousy or the fact some people don't like me.

- Because I look different? Maybe.

- Because I'm taller than the other children – anything different is a target.

- I don't like the feeling that I'm so visible it's impossible not to be seen.

- I find myself sometimes rounding my neck down into my shoulders because I feel it makes me shorter and not a target. But I just end up with a neck ache and my friends tell me I look stupid.

So actually the good bits of being tall are much better than the bad bits.

My mum said that my nan was very tall. She's dead now. I don't remember her. But I've seen photos.

She was this tall and a really classy lady. She was taller than my granddad. I've seen some photos of her and she looks like a model or film star and so full of confidence.

So I guess I should feel like her.

I wonder if she was ever teased at school or was jealous of a giraffe?

Copyright © Naomi Richards and Julia Hague 2016

NOTES TO SUPPORT THE DISCUSSION

Our height depends normally on how tall our parents are, so look at your mum and dad so you can estimate how tall you will be. Genetics are responsible for a lot of how we look.

You need to accept your height and see the benefits and think to yourself that others will catch you up – maybe not now but they will have a growth spurt eventually and may even overtake you.

Height and appearance are not everything. What is inside counts for so much more.

There are many things you can do if your height bothers you. You could ignore the teasers or make a joke out of what they are saying so they feel a bit silly or, if they are stating the obvious, you could agree with them and say, 'Oh so you have noticed I am tall.'

DISCUSSION QUESTIONS TO ASK THE CHILDREN

- What do you think about Victoria's story?

- What do you think about being tall? Why?

- Can you see the advantages?

- What would you say to a friend who does not like being tall?

- If you are tall, have you been teased and what did you do?

ACTIVITIES TO DO WITH THE CHILDREN

HELPING SOMEONE LIKE VICTORIA

What advice would the children give Victoria so she feels okay about being tall? Put the children into twos to discuss and write down what they would say to her. What do they think her response would be to what they said?

ADVANTAGE EXERCISE

Ask the children to write down as many sports as they can think of where height is of benefit.

RESEARCH

Get the children to research a person in the public eye that they consider tall.

LINING UP

Get the children to organize themselves in height order so they can see who is the tallest and who is the smallest. Out of their peer groups they will see that among everyone in the group there are many children of the same height.

BUTTERFLIES, BALLOONS AND ME

(ABOUT HAVING A DISTINGUISHING MARK AND NOT LIKING IT)

MADISON'S STORY

EDUCATORS' NOTES

Suggested age for story – 7–9 years old

Often children are born with an unusual mark somewhere on their face or body. We call it a birthmark, and sometimes they disappear with age and other times they stay with us into adulthood. Given that everyone's skin is different it should be natural to children just to accept that they have a mark and that it is a part of them. However, some children do not feel that way, especially when the mark is noticeable to them and quite prominent on their face. They do not like the mark and wish it would disappear.

We need to give children the confidence to accept their distinguishing mark. If we can, then their self-esteem will rise and they will be able to get on with what they do best. We also need to teach children that any distinguishing feature is what makes a person unique and special.

It is also important to teach children who do not have any particular distinguishing features themselves, not to single out those who do and be cruel to them. Every single person in the world is different and being different is good.

All pre- and post-lesson exercises can be used for evaluation purposes if required.

LEARNING OUTCOMES

- Many people have distinguishing marks.
- Distinguishing marks are a part of who we are and add to our uniqueness.

- Accepting our differences.

- Other people may love our birthmark.

- No one has the right to single out anyone with a physical difference and be unkind to them or make them feel uncomfortable about themselves.

INTRODUCTION STATEMENT

Think about how you look – your face and your body. Do you have something unusual on it that has been there since you were born? Most of us have. Some of you may have lots of freckles in one place or a piece of skin that looks a different colour to the rest of you. Some of you may have something that looks like a shape or have a mark on your skin. Everyone is different in some way physically. Our skin when we are born looks perfect but it is not.

Some of you will have birthmarks and they can be on your body or your face. Birthmarks are just as much a part of you as your belly button, your ears and your feet and we need to make sure that we accept those marks and celebrate them as a part of us. You should never try to hide because of them or wish they were not there. Just as you wouldn't try to hide your curls or your freckles. They are a part of you.

PRE- AND POST-LESSON EXERCISE

Get the children to write down one aspect of their physical selves that they feel makes them unique from everyone else and how they feel about it, and one aspect of a friend's physical self that they think makes them unique. After the story ask the children if they feel any different about either their own or their friend's uniqueness.

Let's read a story about distinguishing marks. Madison, in this story, had a birthmark on her face. She wished it would fly away until someone made her think differently about it.

MADISON'S STORY

When I was very little my mum always used to say that I had my very own butterfly.

It's true. I do. It sits on my cheek.

She also said that it's a special part of who I am. Because it's unique to me.

It's true. No one will ever have a mark that looks exactly like my mark. Ever.

So I guess that's unique. But it doesn't make it special.

I'd rather not have a mark that makes me unique. I'd rather not have a mark at all.

Mum called it a butterfly because it kind of looks like one.

And I think she thought that when I was little, calling it a butterfly made it seem cute.

So if it was cute then I'd like it. I know she meant well. But I didn't like it.

See, butterflies don't sit on your face all day long. Butterflies come and go. Mine doesn't.

And, although it's not huge it is this bright purple colour.

I can see it out of the corner of my eye if I try hard enough.

And I see it as soon as I look in a mirror or catch my reflection in a shop window.

Purple. Well, it is my favourite colour.

But on my face?

How would you like a purple butterfly sitting on your cheek?

Think about it.

All day. And night.

I bet that at first, you'd think that having your own butterfly was amazing.

It might be. For a while. For fun. To have a laugh with your friends.

But always?

Well, I haven't got a choice.

I was born with it.

It started out looking really tiny when I was a baby.

I've seen photos and it looks tiny and paler.

Copyright © Naomi Richards and Julia Hague 2016

Then as I grew it grew with me and got darker.

So it looks much bigger now.

Mum says it's just that the butterfly grew as I grew.

My friend Saanvi says that it's wicked having my own permanent face paint.

And she really does mean it. Saanvi is my best friend.

She agrees with my mum that it looks like a really cool butterfly.

But in reality it's annoying.

See I can't change the face paint.

I can't say today I want to look like a tiger or paint me something else.

I used to think like that all the time about the butterfly.

But then someone I met made me think a bit differently.

Last month I met this boy Dominik at the clinic where I go every year for them to measure the mark and see how it is.

He is a whole lot older than me and he is so cool.

You see he has this balloon-shaped mark across one eye and up onto his forehead.

It's purple, like my mark. But it's much bigger.

And it's perfectly round.

But it's not the balloon that makes him cool. No, it's what he told me.

How he made me feel. About me.

He said sometimes he and his friends mess about and draw different things onto the balloon shape to make it into something else. Like a pair of ears and a tail so it looks like a big fat mouse.

He didn't seem as bothered about his mark as I did about mine.

He grinned when he talked about it.

Dominik said he liked the butterfly on my face.

And when he said that, it did make me smile and he said that when I smiled my butterfly moved its wings.

So I smiled more.

Because I had never known that when I smiled, so did the butterfly. Saanvi had never mentioned it before.

Dominik asked me if the other children at my school ever said things about my mark.

I said that sometimes they did.

Copyright © Naomi Richards and Julia Hague 2016

The mean ones did anyway.

He said that when he first went to secondary school some of the children were mean and said nasty things but he ignored them and in the end they stopped.

He said they got bored with being mean.

He said that his really good friends just accepted the mark on his face as being part of him.

As I was leaving the clinic that day Dominik came over to me and said, 'Madison, don't let anyone tell you how you should feel about yourself. Your mark doesn't make you who you are. Anyone who can't see that, isn't worth being around.'

When I got home I sat on my bed and thought about Dominik and what he had said.

I knew he was right. That being around people who didn't have anything nice to say was pointless. So I decided I'd ignore any ugly comments in future. Just like he had.

I had two great friends, Saanvi and Zofia. And they always said nice things.

He was also right that my mark or butterfly or whatever else anyone called it didn't make me who I was. There was so much more to me. But it was a part of me. I couldn't argue about that.

The doctors at the hospital say that in time I might be able to have the butterfly removed.

Maybe.

One told me that it might fade in time.

Maybe.

When it comes to the time to have it removed I am not sure I'll want to.

By then, I may like being known as the girl with the purple butterfly.

It could be kind of cool.

Like Dominik's balloon is kind of cool.

Copyright © Naomi Richards and Julia Hague 2016

NOTES TO SUPPORT THE DISCUSSION

Madison really did not like having such a large birthmark on her face until she met someone who thought her mark was cool. Dominik had accepted his mark, which looked like a balloon and even had some fun by drawing on it to make it look like different objects. Madison was then able to, with his help, see that her butterfly mark could also do magical things and flap its wings when she smiled. Because Dominik thought her birthmark was cool Madison began to see that hers was not that bad. She began to see that her mark would make her more memorable in other people's eyes, even if that meant being known as the butterfly girl.

We should always try and embrace our unique marks and physical differences and choose to like them rather than disliking them. Disliking them is not going to make them disappear.

Madison also learnt from Dominik that people who say mean things about other people are not worth being around and she decided that she would ignore any ugly comments in future.

No one has the right to make someone else feel bad about themselves so it is best to ignore people who do that. You can't stop people from being mean but you don't have to be around them.

DISCUSSION QUESTIONS TO ASK THE CHILDREN

- What do you think of the story?

- How would you describe the way Madison felt in the beginning?

- How would you describe the way Madison felt at the end?

- How powerful was what Dominik said to Madison?

- Has anyone ever said anything to you that made you change your mind about the way you look? In a good way? In a bad way?

- What do you think about people who try to make others feel bad about themselves?

- Do you think Madison will get the butterfly removed?

ACTIVITIES TO DO WITH THE CHILDREN

CHOOSE YOUR MARK

If the children could choose a really cool birthmark, what would it be, where and why? Get them to write a paragraph about it and draw a picture of the birthmark too.

POWERFUL THOUGHTS

Keeping in mind that we can choose our thoughts, what powerful and positive thoughts could the children have about a physical mark or physical attribute they don't like on themselves? It could be on their face or part of their body. Ask each of the children to write that positive thought in large letters on a piece of paper and cover a blank wall with them.

GAME CHANGER

Get the children to sit in a circle on the floor. Going around the circle get each child to turn to the person on their right and say something that they like about their face. It could be their freckles, teeth, eyes, etc. It must be something that they have that is different to them.

POETRY IN MOTION

Get everyone to write a short poem about Madison and her butterfly and then read a few of them out to the group.

LETTER IN A BOTTLE

Get the children to pretend they are shipwrecked and need to write a short note describing themselves physically for potential rescuers. They must only describe themselves positively and mention anything that distinguishes them from everyone else, such as hair colour or distinguishing marks, etc.

BEING PRETTY IS EVERYTHING...I THINK

(ABOUT REALIZING THAT WHAT YOU'RE MADE TO BELIEVE ISN'T TRUE)

HANNAH'S STORY

EDUCATORS' NOTES

Suggested age for story – 8–11 years old

Children can be very critical of the way they look. Girls are certainly worse than boys. They think that looks are very important and have an idea of what being pretty and perfect is. The story highlights that there is no such thing as perfect and that we all have a different idea of what pretty and good looking is. Once the children are able to see that beauty and good looks are only skin deep, it is hoped they will focus less on the superficial part of who they are and see that it's what's inside that counts. They will focus more on being a kind person who is a good friend/sister/brother.

All pre- and post-lesson exercises can be used for evaluation purposes if required.

LEARNING OUTCOMES

- Children need to be more accepting of the way they look.

- Looking different to other people is a good thing.

- Not everyone is going to see your beauty or good looks.

- We all have something beautiful about us.

- There is no set version of beauty or good looks.

INTRODUCTION STATEMENT

We are going to talk about the way we look today. We can all look in the mirror and be judgemental about what we see. We may not like our nose or think our cheeks are too big, etc. We may want to look like someone else. There is no harm in thinking 'actually I am pretty,' 'I'm really good looking' or 'I am nearly perfect looking' too. If you feel like this, that's great but you don't want to be bragging about how gorgeous you think you are or think you are better looking than anyone else. Not everyone is going to agree with you. Not everyone will see your beauty or good looks the same way that you do, just as you don't see everyone the same way that they see themselves.

PRE- AND POST-LESSON EXERCISE

Ask the children how they feel about the way they look. Get them to write down a sentence about what 'pretty/good looking and perfect' means to them. At the end of the lesson ask them if their statement has changed about what they think pretty/good looking and perfect are.

I am going to share with you Hannah's story. Hannah thought it was the most important thing in the world to be pretty and she focused on looking perfect. One day a girl at school told her she wasn't pretty and after feeling shaken it changed the way she felt about herself. Let's read the story and find out what happened.

HANNAH'S STORY

When I was very little my mum bought me this doll. She had big blue eyes, long eyelashes and beautiful thick hair – a bit like mine – and I thought she was perfect.

Dolls are, of course.

Perfect that is.

I asked my mum only last month why dolls are made to look so perfect. Why don't you ever see a doll with small, narrow eyes or with hair that isn't shiny and soft or one where the eyelashes are short and stubby?

She said that dolls are made that way because manufacturers think that their dolls will sell better if they are pretty and more appealing to boys and girls.

I understood what she meant but surely people can like and play with things that aren't pretty or at least not perfect. Surely?

You can like someone.

Even if they aren't pretty or perfect.

I mean everyone deserves to be liked.

I've never seen a girl in real life…ever…who looks like any of those dolls I've seen. Close maybe…but not exactly like them.

Mum agreed.

She said that it was a good thing that people looked different and didn't look perfect. That no one looked the same, even twins. That looking different and unique was what made us special. That looks weren't everything either. It was what was inside that counted.

I used to think that being pretty was everything. I was told by my aunties and cousins that I was pretty and had better watch out for the boys when I was older. I believed I was. I did not look like a doll but I was nearly perfect in the way I looked.

I said used to.

You see I honestly thought that looking all perfect and having shiny white teeth and a perfect nose and eyes that were big and having eyelashes that batted sweetly at everyone when you spoke, mattered. I thought I had nearly all of those and so I thought that everyone was secretly jealous of me.

Because I was so nearly perfect.

Copyright © Naomi Richards and Julia Hague 2016

And so having people wanting to look like me was really, really important.

At least that's what I thought.

My world was full of posters of perfect-looking pop stars and I spent loads of my spare time flicking through the pages of Mum's magazines and thinking I was nearly as perfect as them.

Not quite but nearly.

My quest to be THE prettiest thing alive filled my waking thoughts and sometimes my dreams.

I didn't concentrate much on my schoolwork.

I didn't think I needed to.

I was going to be a perfect-looking pop star or a model when I left school.

I was working hard on that.

Nothing else mattered.

Then a pretty hard bombshell dropped on me.

I found out I wasn't perfect. Nowhere near it.

Not in everyone's eyes.

And the shock hurt.

And I kind of crumpled inside.

For a while.

Stupidly.

REALLY STUPIDLY.

Because one person said something to me.

Made me feel so bad.

ONE PERSON.

But it felt like the whole world had an opinion.

About me.

Because of her.

She whispered in my ear as I sat in the sun in the corner of the playing field with my friend, Flick.

Laura, this random girl from the year above. A cruel, random girl.

I hadn't paid her any attention. Ever.

But she had obviously noticed me.

She crouched down beside me and leaned across.

Copyright © Naomi Richards and Julia Hague 2016

'Just thought you'd like to know. You've got the ugliest eyes I ever saw. Big, bulgy eyes with spiders clinging onto the ends. You are ugly.'

Then she started laughing. Stood up and walked away towards a group of girls who were laughing.

At me.

Flick went stiff beside me and then looked in my direction.

To see if I was crying. I knew she was waiting to see the tears drop down.

I felt myself going red.

Then I got to my feet as quickly as I could and mumbled something about needing to go to the toilet.

Flick called after me.

I didn't turn around.

I don't know how I got there.

Without crying.

Without making a fool of myself.

Then when I did, I locked the door and stared in the mirror.

I'd always felt confident.

And superior.

Wrongly. I know now.

Because I thought I was so pretty and that meant everything.

It meant I didn't have to work hard at school.

So my grades were rubbish.

Having good looks meant I was more important than everyone else.

But now I wasn't.

Important.

I was a small, deflated balloon ready to be tossed in the rubbish.

I spent the afternoon in lessons trying to concentrate and not get upset.

Walking home from school though, I allowed a tear to shake itself free and fall down my cheek.

I didn't hear the shouting behind me.

Didn't feel the hand on my shoulder until it gripped hard and pulled me up to a stop.

'Flick told me what happened.'

Copyright © Naomi Richards and Julia Hague 2016

Krystle was breathless. She'd been running to catch me up.

I nodded.

I couldn't speak.

'Laura's one of the nastiest people in her class. You didn't believe her did you?'

I nodded again. Couldn't bring the words to my mouth.

I wanted to say that of course I believed her. She told me I was ugly.

But the words wouldn't come out.

Krystle put her arm on my shoulder.

'You're really pretty. I've always wanted to look like you. Your eyes are so beautiful and big and you always look so confident. I wish I could be like that. Don't let Laura make you feel bad.'

I stared blinking at her. SHE thought I was pretty. I thought SHE was pretty too.

'You're really, really pretty.'

I heard the words spill out in a rush towards Krystle.

Krystle looked surprised. Then, embarrassed, she took my hand.

'Listen, we're both worth more than ten of Laura. We are both caring people. We're nice. Laura isn't. She could have kept her thoughts to herself.'

Krystle made sense.

I did cry that night. Let it all out. I decided to leave the posters up in my room though. The pretty smiles, the perfect teeth. I found myself not wanting to be like them anymore. I looked at them and knew I actually was already like them. I had a lovely smile, nice hair and despite what Laura said, my eyes were big and happy. Krystle and I were so different to look at and yet we both liked the way the other looked because we thought the other one was more perfect looking.

But there is no such thing as more perfect.

Perfect isn't a single type of look.

Everyone is different. Everyone.

What and who makes the decision what perfection is?

And actually, does it matter?

I think it's safe to say…no one is perfect. And that is absolutely fine.

In fact it's simply…perfection.

Copyright © Naomi Richards and Julia Hague 2016

NOTES TO SUPPORT THE DISCUSSION

It is hard when how you feel about yourself is questioned by another person. You feel amazing, possibly superior to others, because of your looks and then someone decides to make you feel rubbish. We need to try and not let it affect us. After all, it is their opinion. We need to put more emphasis on what we are inside rather than how we look, and if someone is mean to us we need to say something clever back and make sure that their words do not hurt us.

DISCUSSION QUESTIONS TO ASK THE CHILDREN

- How do you feel about Hannah?

- Has anyone ever said anything about the way you look in a nasty way? How did it make you feel? Did you say anything bad?

- If it hasn't happened to you, has it happened to a friend of yours? How did you support them?

- Do you think it is important what other people think of you – especially those who are not friends of yours?

- Do you think that the people you see on TV or in magazines look perfect?

- What does 'perfect' mean to you?

ACTIVITIES TO DO WITH THE CHILDREN

QUALITIES THAT MAKE YOU ATTRACTIVE

Get each child to write down five things that can make someone attractive without mentioning the way they look.

ROLE MODELS

Get the children to think of a role model who they believe works hard but is not perfect. Get them to share the person and their reason with the group.

GIVING COMPLIMENTS

Ask the children to look at the person next to them. What do they admire about their face or body? Ask them to share with one another what they admire.

STRAIGHT-TALKING SENTENCES

Using the letters from the word 'PERFECT', can the children make up sentences about the important traits they have? There must be no mention of looks.

CHAMELEONS AND STICK INSECTS

(ABOUT BEING DIFFERENT TO EVERYONE ELSE AND WANTING TO HIDE IT)

ADRIAN'S STORY

EDUCATORS' NOTES

Suggested age for story – 7–10 years old

Children want to blend in. They do not want to be noticed for being different. Of course we all are and some differences can be easy to hide. However, when you have a more marked physical difference – not just the length or colour of your hair, for example – it can be very difficult to hide. There are many children who are born with a disability and they are never too sure of the reaction they are going to receive from other children. It can be scary for the child with the disability because they know there will be children, and possibly adults, who will stare. Some of them may even make comments about how they look.

Children who have a disability need to feel empowered to not feel embarrassed and to be proud of who they are. They also need to feel supported by their friends and other children in their class or school. If they can get over their negative thoughts and worries then they will be able to hold their head up high and not care what others may think.

Those in the child's peer group have a huge role to play in how they feel about themselves and it's important that other children know about their pivotal role.

All pre- and post-lesson exercises can be used for evaluation purposes if required.

LEARNING OUTCOMES

- Accept other people's physical differences.

- Never want to be anything other than what you are.

- Be proud of who you are.

- Challenge any negative feelings you may have about yourself or others.

- Be supportive to anyone you meet who may have physical or other challenges in their life.

INTRODUCTION STATEMENT

Every one of us is different. Look around and see. We all have different coloured skin and hair colour and length. Some of you are tall and some smaller. Some have blue eyes, some have brown and some green. The range of differences in the way people look all around the world is truly amazing. How we look is different, just like who we are inside is different. What matters most is what is inside.

On the outside some children are born with a physical difference or disability. Just because they do, it should not have an effect on how we feel about them. We should help support anyone who is struggling with how they feel about themselves because of their disability. We need to treat them the same as everyone else.

If we are the person who has a noticeable physical difference we need to learn to accept this is a part of who we are and not hide it. If others are cruel to us about it then they are not our true friend as friends are kind and accepting.

PRE- AND POST-LESSON EXERCISE

Ask the children what their thoughts are when they look at someone who has a disability. After the story ask them the same. Have their views changed?

Adrian, in this story, has something called clubfoot, which means that one leg can be shorter than the other. He felt very self-conscious about it and tried to hide it. Let's see if he overcame his embarrassment.

ADRIAN'S STORY

I used to spend ages and ages staring at the stick insects in our science lab at school. I loved that they could hide so easily from you. Become invisible.

Did you know that a stick insect's name means 'apparition'? My dad said that means a ghost and it's because they resemble sticks. So they're really difficult to see sitting on branches.

What Dad doesn't know is that I really wanted to be a stick insect.

So I could hide away from interested eyes.

And then life would have been easier.

At least I thought that.

Until I met this boy.

His name was Aarav.

And getting to know him showed me that hiding wasn't what I should do at all.

I was born with something called 'clubfoot'. It means I have a wonky foot.

My dad had it when he was little too.

It can run in families.

Dad never talked to me about how he felt with his clubfoot.

I wish he had.

But dad wasn't very talkative about that sort of thing.

So I never asked.

I had an operation when I was little to correct my foot and then wore special boots attached to each other with a bar.

I remember having to wear the boots at night right up until the end of reception.

When all my friends were starting to have sleepovers I never did. And I didn't go to them either.

You see, Mum never invited any other children to stay over because I told her I was embarrassed about my boots, and I never wanted to take my boots with me to a sleepover.

So when the boots went and I did get my first sleepover I was so excited and Mum invited more than one boy to stay.

Copyright © Naomi Richards and Julia Hague 2016

But one of them was not nice.

Ryan.

He saw my smaller foot and shorter leg when we were getting ready for bed.

And he made a nasty comment.

He made me feel sad.

I was six, and nasty, mean comments make you cry when you are six.

I found Mum and cried.

She hugged me when I told her what Ryan had said.

She said not to worry about mean people.

That my foot and leg weren't that noticeable.

The usual things that mothers say.

But the comments from Ryan stuck with me.

I only limp a little bit. Sometimes.

I try not to. So that no one will take notice of me.

But sometimes I get tired. So I limp.

I always tried to wear long trousers too. Even in the summer, so no one would see my leg.

And I hated sports when the weather got warmer because then I had to wear shorts.

I felt very self-conscious.

Until Aarav, a new boy at school, and I became really good friends.

He came straight up to me the day he arrived and said 'hello' and started asking me questions.

Mrs Davis, our teacher, saw us talking together and decided to put Aarav next to me in class.

'Take care of Aarav will you, Adrian? Help him settle in.'

But it wasn't me taking care of Aarav. Within a week Aarav had taken care of me.

Of how I felt.

Aarav invited me to his house for tea.

It was a warm and sunny afternoon and I could see that Aarav's family had a large inflatable swimming pool in the garden.

Two girls were sitting in it.

Copyright © Naomi Richards and Julia Hague 2016

They were a lot older than us. Aarav introduced them to me as his sister Shefali and her friend Ella.

Aarav thought it would be a great idea to join them.

I heard Aarav offer to lend me some swimming trunks as he went back inside.

I heard the words as I stood alone.

In a single second, my heart had gone from singing happily at the friendship and fun we were having to realizing that if I wanted to go into the pool, everyone would see my foot and leg.

Then something special happened.

Shefali's friend Ella stood up and reached down for Shefali's arms.

She hauled her up to her feet and still holding onto her reached outside of the pool.

Hidden behind the pool were two crutches.

Shefali took the crutches and then moved off, dragging one foot behind her, towards the house.

'We'll let you boys have the pool to yourselves,' Shefali said as she turned around and smiled.

'You'll end up messing about and splashing us anyway and we're going to a party so we don't want you messing our hair up,' Ella added giggling.

I bet you're thinking that the special thing was that I didn't have to show my foot and leg to the girls after all.

No, you're wrong.

The special thing was watching Shefali totally at ease with whatever it was that was wrong with her leg.

And Ella was too.

They just got on with whatever they were going to do.

And the fact that she didn't care about me seeing her.

That was the most special thing of all.

So I changed into the swimming trunks in their little summerhouse when Aarav came back and I climbed into the swimming pool without looking at him.

But Aarav never said anything. If he noticed my leg or my foot he obviously didn't care.

Copyright © Naomi Richards and Julia Hague 2016

And I didn't ask him about Shefali.

Because it didn't matter.

And I realized that my short leg and small foot didn't really matter either.

So from that day on my attitude changed. About myself.

I stopped wanting to be a stick insect. Hiding from everyone was stupid.

Sure there were always going to be mean people like Ryan. Who would try to make me feel bad about myself.

But letting a person who is mean affect who I am is pretty stupid too.

So for now I'm focusing on being a chameleon.

Chameleons can blend in with their surroundings but they don't necessarily hide.

So while I'm not quite ready to parade myself in front of everyone like a peacock, I'm certainly not going to hide from the world.

Because I've got so much to offer and if I was a stick insect no one would see what that is.

Copyright © Naomi Richards and Julia Hague 2016

NOTES TO SUPPORT THE DISCUSSION

Adrian was very self-conscious of his leg until two things happened. The first was Shefali's attitude to her own leg and her disability. Once Adrian saw that she was fine with it and did not make a fuss about using crutches or dragging her foot along the floor his mindset changed. The second was that because Aarav did not mention Adrian's leg then he did not say anything either. His coping mechanism was not to look at his friend so that he did not have to have direct eye contact. That would have helped. Often when we are embarrassed we tend to look away so we do not have to see the other person's reaction.

Aarav was a good friend. He liked Adrian for who he was.

Adrian, after the swimming pool incident, decided he no longer wanted to be a stick insect. He realized that if people were going to be cruel then they would be. That letting a cruel comment change the way you felt about yourself was silly. Although we cannot stop people from being cruel, Adrian realized that it was more important to be himself and not hide away.

Self-confidence can be infectious. Shefali passed that on to Adrian. When we see someone cope well in a situation, we can then question why we aren't coping and learn from that person.

DISCUSSION QUESTIONS TO ASK THE CHILDREN

- What do you think of Adrian's story?

- Do you think he did the right thing?

- Would you feel the same if you were Adrian?

- What do you think about him wanting to be a stick insect?

- What did you think of the way Shefali handled her disability?

- How should you treat someone with a disability?

- What would be an unkind thing to do?

- How would you help someone like Adrian to feel better about himself?

ACTIVITIES TO DO WITH THE CHILDREN

TYPES OF DISABILITY

There are lots of different types of physical disability. Get the children to research and then choose one to write about so they have a better understanding of what it is.

STANDING UP TO RYAN

Get the children to write a letter to Ryan that defends Adrian. They need to share their thoughts on what was wrong about what he did.

BEING CONFIDENT LIKE SHEFALI

Why do the children think Shefali is like she is? What kind of thoughts and attitude do they think she has? Get the children to shout out their answers.

POSTER ART

Get the children to design a poster that is about embracing the way people look and their disability.

GETTING AHEAD

Disability isn't a barrier to doing anything in life. Get the children to research someone in the public eye who has a disability and has achieved success and write about them.

Part 2

PUBERTY

STORY SEVEN

PE BLUES

(ABOUT NOT LIKING HAVING TO CHANGE IN FRONT OF OTHERS)

ALEX'S STORY

EDUCATORS' NOTES

Suggested age for story – 11 years old (end of Year 6)

Children need to be aware that other children may have negative body image. They also need to know what changes take place in puberty. This story touches on these two issues. It encourages children to think more about how other friends may feel about their bodies and be more sensitive about what they say to them. It also teaches children about body changes that happen. If children are aware of the changes they will be more accepting of them when they happen and keep their confidence high. This confidence will help them in friendships and at school.

All pre- and post-lesson exercises can be used for evaluation purposes if required.

LEARNING OUTCOMES

- Children to be more accepting of their body.
- To have positive body image.
- To be confident when changing in front of others.
- To understand how others may feel about their own body.
- To realize that everyone is going through the same changes.

INTRODUCTION STATEMENT

Today we are going to talk about body issues and how sometimes we don't feel great about our bodies. Our bodies are always changing when we are children and this is part of growing up.

It can sometimes be a bit embarrassing having to let classmates see parts of your body when undressing, especially when you start to get hairy under your arms and maybe get a bit smelly.

When you have PE and you need to get changed there is no choice. Changing in front of other children even when they are your friends can make you feel very self-conscious, worried and scared especially if you are going through puberty.

PRE- AND POST-LESSON EXERCISE

Ask the children to write down a sentence about how they feel about their body pre-story. Are they confident about their body and do they mind changing in front of their friends? Ask them to write another sentence about how they feel after they've listened to the story to see if their thoughts have changed.

I am going to share with you Alex's story. Alex did not like PE because he did not like changing in front of other people.

ALEX'S STORY

I HATE PE.

No really. I do.

Not because I'm no good at it, because I really ace it. Mostly.

I even beat Ricky at the 100 metres last month.

No, it's not because I'm no good.

It's because before the PE lesson, there's this horror to go through.

You know. The horror of getting changed.

The whole taking my clothes off.

The whole getting into my PE kit.

When we're all in the changing rooms elbowing each other for space.

Trying to get changed.

Not like the others are really remotely interested in looking at me or anything.

I mean I know that.

I do.

But sometimes I wonder if they have glanced at me.

You know maybe by accident but then they might go on looking.

Comparing themselves to me.

Because I know I do that too.

Compare myself to them.

Are they growing hair where I am?

Am I so abnormal or are we all the same really?

You can sometimes see it out of the corner of your eye.

You don't have to stare.

And then there's the fact that no matter what I do…I kind of smell when I get sweaty.

Like my armpits do.

And okay, yes I know the other boys smell a bit too sometimes.

You notice it as everyone strips off and gets into their kit.

Copyright © Naomi Richards and Julia Hague 2016

I'm so aware that I stink that sometimes I pull my school sweater off and grab my PE shirt and try and get it on fast enough to stop the smell from getting up my friends' noses.

I've tried turning my back on the others and going into a far corner where there's not too many other kids. Then I can rush the whole taking off one set of clothes and hauling on the PE kit as fast as I can.

Trouble is I'm not fast enough and trying to be fast just makes everything go wrong. So what normally happens is I get all tangled up and end up hopping around losing my balance when I'm trying to rush.

Which of course brings more attention to me.

Then there's the whole making an excuse to go to the toilet and then quickly trying to change in there, before the teacher notices.

I tried it once.

I got in the toilet, took my clothes off and then realized to my horror that I'd left my kit in my bag and would have to either run out with nothing on or change back into my school uniform and rescue the kit and start all over again.

Yep you guessed it. I chose to put everything back on and go back into the changing room to get the kit. By that time everyone was ready and I got a good telling off from Mr Channing. He told me I was being slow and lazy and had to hurry up so I swallowed hard and changed fast, willing every second to pass fast because I knew the whole class was standing there waiting…and of course now they were looking and if my armpits were as smelly as I thought they were…oh man.

Epic fail.

I stand in front of the bathroom mirror sometimes and look at myself. Without my clothes on. I know there are changes going on. I'm not blind. I can see. And I'm scared.

But I'm a boy. I'm not supposed to feel like that. Am I?

I mean scared is supposed to be a wussy thing to be. Seriously.

But what if I grow up to be abnormal? What if everything isn't the same as everyone else's once my body has done its growing thing? What if I'm doomed to have hairy, smelly armpits forever?

What if they get worse and worse and in the end I look like a gorilla and smell worse?

It's really scary. It doesn't make sense. What I think.

Copyright © Naomi Richards and Julia Hague 2016

I mean I haven't seen any men who look and smell like gorillas. But it still scares me.

Life was so easy before my body started to do these things. I didn't mind jumping in the paddling pool with my best mate, Joe, a few years ago in the garden. With no clothes on!

Imagine that! Me with no clothes on. No smelly parts of my body. No hair. Not caring because I didn't realize that our bodies could change. I looked the same as Joe and he looked the same as me. Simple. Nothing complicated.

Mum and Dad have told me over and over again that I'm developing normally. That everything is fine. Dad even had that talk with me. You know the one about body changes and girls and stuff. The teacher at school who does PSHE has given us the talk about our bodies changing too. About how natural it all is.

But I'm still scared.

The whole getting undressed thing sucks.

I've noticed recently…not that I have gone out of my way staring or anything, that quite a few of the boys in my class are getting changed faster than they used to. I wonder if they worry about their smelly armpits.

I talked to Joe about it.

He said he didn't worry about his armpits. But he did say his feet were getting really smelly and he hated changing into his trainers in the changing room.

I haven't noticed his smelly feet. But then he says he hasn't noticed my armpits.

Dad said we all think what we have is worse than anyone else. My smelly armpits might worry me, but Joe's feet drive him nuts. For all I know Ricky thinks he smells or something but I've never thought about him or noticed.

Dad's right. I guess. I beat myself up about thinking stupid thoughts. But my brain is still obsessed with gorillas.

I dreamt about the jungle last night. Go figure.

Copyright © Naomi Richards and Julia Hague 2016

NOTES TO SUPPORT THE DISCUSSION

Your body changing is a good thing. It is preparing itself to become a young man or woman. Every living thing goes through physical change as it grows into an adult. Remember that.

You don't need to be afraid or worried about what other people think of your body. Your friends will all go through this change although it may not be at the same time as you. Children develop at different rates. We all end up vaguely the same in the end.

One thing you could do, if you feel embarrassed, is to change near those people you call good friends and know you can trust, who are not going to comment on the way your body looks and smells. You could even tell them how scared you feel – they may say they feel the same.

If you are really worried about your body changing – the hair and sweatiness – talk to your mum, dad or friends if you are able to. Mums and Dads always have great advice and will have been through the same when they were young.

DISCUSSION QUESTIONS TO ASK THE CHILDREN

- What advice would you give to Alex?

- How do you feel about PE and changing in front of other people?

- How can you feel proud of your changing body?

- What can you do from a hygiene point of view to take care of your body and its changes?

- If you could not share your feelings with Mum or Dad, who else could you talk to?

ACTIVITIES TO DO WITH THE CHILDREN

HELPING SOMEONE LIKE ALEX

Get the children to answer the question, 'How do we recognize someone is embarrassed and how can we help them feel more at ease?' Ask each child to write ideas on post-its for each question and then place them on two sheets of paper at the front of the group.

POSITIVE PE THOUGHTS

Give out sheets of paper with a picture of a child and a thought bubble coming out of their head drawn on each one. Ask the children to write a positive thought the child could have to make them feel more confident about their body.

LOVE YOUR BODY

Ask the children to write a letter to themselves about their body and mention the bits they love.

LOOKING AFTER YOUR BODY

Get the children into groups of four. Give out one sheet of paper to each group with a large outline of a child on it. Ask them to discuss in groups and then write within the outline how that child could look after themselves. There may be lots of ways they had not thought about before (using deodorant, changing clothes frequently, brushing their teeth daily, drinking water, eating well). Once they have finished, ask the groups to call out their answers and write them on the board. The groups can see how many they got on their drawing.

FOLLOW-ON PUBERTY EXERCISE

Using an outline drawing of a boy and an outline drawing of a girl get the children to call out changes that each will go through as they go through puberty. It will raise laughs and giggling but should be informative.

CHANGES

(ABOUT PERIODS AND OTHER GROWING UP MILESTONES)

CHARLOTTE'S STORY

EDUCATORS' NOTES

Suggested age for story – girls 10–11 years old

Children grow up very fast. Puberty seems to start at around 10 or 11 in some girls and a girl's period will start sometime after her body starts to develop. Of course, there is no specific age but a girl knows she is growing into a woman because she can see and feel her body is changing. Once a girl can embrace that this is what is going to happen she will become more relaxed and won't panic when she gets her first period because she will be ready.

Going forward she will have more of an idea when it will come on a monthly basis and therefore will be more aware of her moods. This will allow her to plan for it, giving her the confidence to deal with her period when it starts. Being aware of how a period can make her feel and the ways in which she can cope with any discomfort will also mean that periods won't prevent her from carrying on as normal in the rest of her daily life.

It's important to encourage girls to talk to others in their friendship groups about their periods so that they can support one another with something that is a normal part of growing into a young woman.

All pre- and post-lesson exercises can be used for evaluation purposes if required.

LEARNING OUTCOMES

- Be prepared for your first period.
- Do not worry when you get your first period.

- Tell someone you can trust to help if you get caught out.

- Recognize your moods and if you feel grumpy tell your closest friends why.

- Learn how to manage any discomfort you might feel during your period.

- Realize that all the girls in your class will at some time experience the same as you.

INTRODUCTION STATEMENT

Reaching puberty can be a very scary thing. There will be changes to your body that you may not like but in order to become a young lady they have to happen. We all need to grow hair in strange places and periods are essential for later on in life when you want to have a baby. Do not be scared of these changes. Your friends will all be going through the same thing as you.

You can make it easier by preparing for your first period and also it could be good to talk to your friends or mum about how you feel. Even if you are not prepared there will always be someone on hand to help you through the tummy ache, etc.

PRE- AND POST-LESSON EXERCISE

Ask the girls how they feel about getting their first period before the story. Ask them again after the story. How differently do they feel now?

Today we are going to hear about Charlotte and what happened when she started her period. She was not as prepared for it as she had hoped she would be. Did everything work out in the end? Let's read her story.

CHARLOTTE'S STORY

It happened when I was least expecting it.

Mum had prepared me for it. Our teacher had told us about it. My friend Sabine had told me how it had happened to her.

But I'd forgotten.

Seriously.

I know you're going to wonder how on earth I could forget about it. Not be prepared.

I'm nearly 11. It could have happened any day soon. Or not. A bit like a lottery. You never quite knew when.

But I was busy that day. Really busy.

I'd run out of the house in the morning, shoving toast into my mouth as my lift sounded her horn impatiently, throwing my homework exercise books into my school bag.

I didn't notice that the night before I'd taken absolutely everything out of the bag to find a coloured marker pen and hadn't put everything back.

I didn't notice that the small purse that had the necessary items in it was left on my bedroom floor.

So I sat in class in blissful ignorance of what was about to happen.

I'd had a bit of a tummy ache that morning when I woke up.

Nothing special. A grumbling ache, on and off.

I had an important test in maths that day so I didn't tell Mum. I was scared she'd keep me off school.

Besides I didn't feel sick or anything.

But after the maths test the stomach ache grabbed my attention again.

Together with a headache.

The hockey match that I was in the next day was an important one.

I couldn't be sick.

In science class Sabine leaned across and asked me in a whisper if I was okay.

I snapped at her that I was fine.

That surprised me a bit. That I'd snapped at my best friend like that.

Copyright © Naomi Richards and Julia Hague 2016

She gave me a bit of a hurt look and went back to her work.

By lunchtime the tummy ache was more than an occasional dull ache. It ached all the time.

I took myself off to the toilet.

There it was.

The reason for the tummy ache. The headache. The snapping at my best friend.

My very first period.

Sneaky. Taken me by surprise.

Even though it was something we all talked about. Waited for.

It had snuck up on me.

But I was prepared, wasn't I?

I had all the things I needed in my school bag. So I fetched my bag and searched around inside. For the towels my mum had given me. And the fresh underwear.

Nothing.

I felt panicked.

Just for a second.

Then a voice behind me took away my panic in an instance.

It was Sabine.

She hadn't been put off by me being snappy.

She was concerned for me. She was my best friend.

I told her what had happened and she smiled and pulled her own school bag over to me.

She handed me a towel and her own fresh underwear and gave me this big hug.

'If you ever get stuck, Mrs Connors, the School Nurse, always has some,' she said.

The headache and tummy ache didn't last long. My first period didn't either. And I found that as soon as my period started I stopped being snappy.

I've learnt that a warm bath or warm hot water bottle really helps with my tummy ache.

And that when I get super grumpy I know my period is due soon.

I've also started getting spots on my face just before my period.

Copyright © Naomi Richards and Julia Hague 2016

I haven't had many of them but I know they are a part of my life as I'm growing up.

Sabine and I have a code between us. We say 'it's that time again' whenever either of us starts our period to let the other person know why they are miserable.

Sabine and I have also noticed that we have bits of hair growing under our arms and down at the front.

Our bodies are going through changes.

We both need to shower more because our bodies do smell a bit if we don't.

I know boys go through changes too. Our teacher has told us about all the changes that we go through when we are growing.

I'm glad my mum prepared me for the biggest one in a girl's life.

And I'm glad my friend is sharing it with me as we both grow up.

Changes are part of growing up.

It's exciting.

Copyright © Naomi Richards and Julia Hague 2016

NOTES TO SUPPORT THE DISCUSSION

Every girl will feel differently about going through puberty. Charlotte seemed quite calm but was not as prepared as she could have been when she got her period. Some girls may be frightened that it will come and everyone will know about it. They won't. You can be so discreet about your period. Your friends don't need to know unless you want them to.

If you are worried then perhaps your mum, an auntie or a friend's mum could be someone to talk to. They would be able to answer your questions and help in any way.

Becoming a woman needs to be embraced. If you are one of the first amongst your friends perhaps you can reassure them about any fears they have when it happens to them. You can be the person full of advice.

DISCUSSION QUESTIONS TO ASK THE CHILDREN

- What do you think of Charlotte's story?

- What did she learn about herself?

- How do you feel about entering puberty?

- What are you most scared of?

- How do you feel about becoming a woman?

- Who would you speak to about your feelings?

- What advice would you give a friend who is worried about starting her periods?

ACTIVITIES TO DO WITH THE CHILDREN

BE A DESIGNER
Ask the girls to design a pack of things for girls that they would find useful so they are prepared for their first period.

INFORMATION LEAFLET
Get the girls into groups and ask them to put together a leaflet for girls that will tell them everything they need to know about puberty.

MAKE A LIST

Ask the girls to put together a list of everything they do in their lives that shouldn't stop just because they have a period.

BE AN AGONY AUNT

Ask the girls to imagine that they are an agony aunt for a teen magazine. They have had a letter from a girl who is worried about starting her periods. Get them to write a letter back to her telling her all the things she can do to prepare for them.

Part 3

SELF-ESTEEM AND SELF-WORTH

I'M NOT LIKE HER...OR HER... OR HER, SO I DON'T LIKE ME

(ABOUT WORKING OUT WHY YOU DON'T LIKE YOURSELF AND CHANGING YOUR MIND)

LAUREN'S STORY

EDUCATORS' NOTES

Suggested age for story – 9–11 years old

Children need to learn to accept who they are, warts and all. They need to appreciate who they are and not want to be anyone else. Once children have accepted who they are they will feel more confident and comfortable in their skin, which will have a knock-on effect on their confidence. When children feel more confident they are able to do more and have healthier relationships.

All pre- and post-lesson exercises can be used for evaluation purposes if required.

LEARNING OUTCOMES

- Appreciate who you are.
- Don't try to be anyone else.
- Your friends admire things about you but might not always say it.
- Share your negative feelings about yourself with someone you trust.

INTRODUCTION STATEMENT

Our topic for today is about working out why we sometimes don't like ourselves and how we can turn those negative feelings into positive ones with the help of friends. We are all different but we all have something we admire about our friends. Our friends also have things they admire about us too. Never be tempted to want to change because if you do change you won't be the person you were meant to be and your friends will think, 'What has happened to my friend?'

One of the hardest things about growing up is the way your looks change. We need to remember that we are still the same person inside. Our faces do change – they mature and that is a good thing.

PRE- AND POST-LESSON EXERCISE

Ask the children if they like who they are and how they deal with wanting to change parts of themselves. Get them to listen to the story and then ask them to write down a sentence about how they could now think differently about wanting to change who they are.

I am going to share Lauren's story. At first she was more focused on what everyone else looked like and how they were, rather than appreciating who she was. In the end, though, Lauren began to change her thoughts about herself. Let's find out how and why.

LAUREN'S STORY

Why is it that when we are tiny we don't care what other people are like, we just get on with playing and eating and rushing around with other kids but when we get to school we start looking at the other kids and wishing we could be different or like them?

The ones we want to be with. The ones we don't.

The ones we want to be like. The ones we don't.

I mean it doesn't make any sense.

We haven't changed.

We're still the same child we were.

What happens inside our heads?

Is there a switch somewhere that kind of goes on and makes us look at ourselves and then look at everyone around us and compare?

The comparison switch?

I know I'm ten but I can still remember playgroup.

The sandpit, the tiny slide, the rushing around with other little kids and just…having fun. I remember all that. It makes me feel warm to remember.

What I don't remember was in any way feeling that I wanted to be… not me.

I was just getting used to being me.

I was kind of testing everything, if that makes sense. You know, walking and running and jumping and letting sand run through my fingers and listening to sounds.

I looked in the mirror and saw a smiling kid and so I smiled back. I loved me. I remember seeing a video of me kissing the mirror at my own reflection.

So why do I feel so horrible about the reflection I see in the mirror now I am bigger?

The ten-year-old me.

The longer haired, freckly faced, disapproving me.

Why don't I want to be me, but need to be someone else?

I don't know when it started.

Copyright © Naomi Richards and Julia Hague 2016

I really don't.

I think I was okay for the first couple of years at school.

At least I don't remember feeling bad about myself at all.

I just got on with fitting in somehow. Getting myself into a group of friends.

At five and six you care more about the birthday parties you are getting invited to and how long it is until Christmas than you care about looking or being like someone else.

Then at about seven or eight I guess I started analysing why one girl was friends with another and I think for the first time in my life I felt jealous.

It wasn't a nice feeling I can tell you that.

It hurts. Like inside. Like a real pain.

But being jealous of what?

My mum talked for ages with me about it.

We finally worked out what I was really jealous about. There was a girl at school who I wanted more than anything else to be MY friend but she was friends with someone else and not me.

I dreamt of how much fun the other girl would be to hang around with.

Mum tried to reason with me that I didn't know the other girl at all so she might be boring or not as exciting as I thought.

But I had built her up so much in my head as being this special, fun-loving kid that I couldn't believe I was wrong.

I wanted to be like her.

I wanted to be like the girls who were friends with her.

More than anything else, I didn't want to be me.

I resented ME. Because I obviously wasn't fun and I certainly wasn't THEM.

Then…bam…one day the girl left. Her parents moved away.

The girl who had been her friend returned to being around me again and life returned to normal.

But that feeling.

The 'I'm not good enough' feeling wouldn't shake.

So the more I looked at the girls around me I felt more and more that I wanted to be like them and not like me.

Copyright © Naomi Richards and Julia Hague 2016

I stopped looking in the mirror because there was no way I could change the image staring back.

I tried dressing differently but no one commented at school so I came home and threw the new clothes onto the bed in a strop and just cried.

Then, about two months ago one of my friends came over to stay the night.

Mum told us not to stay up late and lights off at 10 pm.

Of course the lights did go off but we sat huddled together with a torch and whispered quietly into the night.

My friend's name was Cara.

What she did for me that night…well I guess all I can say is that I owe her…big time.

We got talking about how we felt about the future and ourselves and we giggled a lot about our plans. Mine to work anywhere where a boat or water is involved and hers to be someone who works in the City like her dad in some big bank or something.

It all seemed a long way off.

Dreams.

Then we got talking about us. About our bodies. Our hair. Our eyes.

Then I started crying.

I don't know why it happened.

I think that I just felt safe talking to Cara and it all came flooding out.

I told her I hated my face and couldn't do anything with my long curly hair.

I told her I wanted to have long straight hair that shone like it did on the adverts for shampoos and that I wanted to have every single freckle taken away and have perfect skin like I saw in the magazines.

I wanted to be tall like Georgina at school and have a nose like Sascha and be thin like Rachel and have legs like Marta.

I wanted to be anyone rather than be me.

Then she just looked at me and started laughing.

Well sniggering quietly since we were supposed to be asleep.

At first I was so shocked.

I'd poured out my heart to her and she was laughing at me.

Then she grabbed my hand and told me something I won't ever forget.

Copyright © Naomi Richards and Julia Hague 2016

She said that she had always wanted to look like ME. That she had always wanted to be like Zoe and make everyone laugh. That coming and having a sleepover with me was such fun.

She said that her mum had told her that everyone wants to look like someone else. Everyone.

That no one is perfect. That no one likes themselves totally.

That everyone has something that someone else wants. It might be their legs, their eyes or their hair.

But her mum told her that you can only be you.

You're born you. Not another person.

That if we were all alike it would be a very boring…and very confusing world.

So wanting to be like someone else is like saying to yourself that you don't like being the person you were born as.

And I nodded.

It made sense.

What surprised me the most was that Cara had always wanted to look like ME.

This is the ME that I didn't want to look like and someone else wanted it!

So if you're hearing this and feeling like you don't like yourself.

If you're hearing this and feel that being or looking like someone else is better – think this…

That somewhere out there is a person who would love to be you. Would love to look like you. Wants to be like you.

How strange is that?

And so hold on to what you look like. Hold on to what you are.

Because you're the only one who can be you.

Yeah. Now that's kind of wow.

Copyright © Naomi Richards and Julia Hague 2016

NOTES TO SUPPORT THE DISCUSSION

Children often think that being someone else is much better than being themselves. They may think they aren't as interesting or attractive as another child and so they spend their time wanting to change who they are rather than accepting who they are. They may also focus on being jealous of an individual and this can take over their lives.

It's important for children to realize that they shouldn't be jealous of their friends or others and want to be like them in either looks or the way they appear to be. There will probably be other children who look at them and want to be like them too. If they can learn to embrace the fact that everyone is different and has different qualities they will realize that they too have unique qualities and will learn to love instead of criticize themselves.

The signs of knowing that a child does not like themselves are visible through the language they use. They often criticize themselves or say how wonderful everyone else is. They may shy away from being around some people who make them feel inferior or even shy away from their peers.

DISCUSSION QUESTIONS TO ASK THE CHILDREN

- What are your thoughts about Lauren?

- What advice would you have given her?

- Why do you think she doubted who she was?

- What do you think about being jealous of your friends?

- How do you notice when your friend does not like who they are? What are the signs?

- If a friend told you they did not like themselves what would you do?

ACTIVITIES TO DO WITH THE CHILDREN

ADVICE COLUMN

Ask the children to write a letter to a fictional friend who is not happy with how they look and persuade that friend that they are in fact just fine the way they are.

POSITIVE THOUGHTS

What positive thoughts should someone have when a negative thought pops into their head about who they are? Ask the children to make a list of five and then get them to shout them out and write them on the board. These positive thoughts can be collated into a handout for the children to keep.

INTO THE FUTURE

Ask the children to draw a portrait of how they expect to look in the future. Get them to appreciate that our faces and bodies change.

TWO BY TWO

Ask the children to pair up and face each other. Each person in the pair has five minutes to tell the other what they really like and appreciate about the other.

TALENT SHOW

(ABOUT FEELING LIKE YOU'RE USELESS AT EVERYTHING WHEN YOU ARE NOT)

NOAH'S STORY

EDUCATORS' NOTES

Suggested age for story – 10–11 years old

Children need to learn not to second-guess what others are thinking about them. Second-guessing can change the way children feel about themselves and it can lower their self-esteem. It does this by planting negative thoughts in their heads about who they are. We never know what someone thinks about us unless we ask them.

We need to be confident about who we are and we should not hide our talents. Children should share their talents with others so that others can learn from them. This will increase their self-esteem and make them feel good. Children also need to understand that just because they are not knowledgeable in a certain area, it does not make them talentless.

All children need to be encouraged to try new things, to develop and nurture talents and see what they are good at. Trying new things will help them to develop a wider range of skills and breadth of life experience. We also need to teach children that sometimes they will not be great at something, and that is all right, because no one is good at everything.

All pre- and post-lesson exercises can be used for evaluation purposes if required.

LEARNING OUTCOMES

- Do not guess what others think about you.
- Everyone has talents – be brave and share them.

- Try new things.

- Don't be afraid of failing at something.

- No one is good at everything.

INTRODUCTION STATEMENT

What other people think of us is not as important as what we think about ourselves. We need to recognise what we are good at and what we are not so good at. We also need to not second-guess what others think about us. For example, if you don't do well in a maths test there is no reason to think that everyone must think you are stupid. That thought may not have crossed their mind because they know you are smart in other areas.

Show off your talents and let others learn from you in the subjects that you do know lots about and when it comes to trying new things you will never know how good you are unless you try. Have the confidence to say to yourself, 'I may be great at this so I need to have a go, and if I don't do well the first time, then I can practise and get better. If I try something several times and I don't get better it doesn't matter.'

No one person is good at everything. Remember that. Who wants to be perfect anyway?

PRE- AND POST-LESSON EXERCISE

Before reading the story ask the children what stops them showing off their talents? Get them to share their thoughts. After the story get them to share how they now think about sharing their talents.

Let's read about Noah who was scared to show off his knowledge and to try new things. It seems the thoughts in his head were stopping him.

NOAH'S STORY

I used to think I knew what people thought about me.

I used to think that everyone thought I was useless.

I don't know why I thought it.

Maybe it was because I was last at a lot of things at school.

Or maybe because I never seemed to get picked for anything.

So I got it into my head that at school they thought I couldn't do anything.

That I was useless.

But what I didn't know was that they didn't think that at all.

And they didn't understand why I hid my talents from them at school.

Or why I always got bad marks or didn't turn up to try for sport or school plays.

Then one day things changed.

My school friends and the teachers saw the real me. The out-of-school me.

The me who hangs out with my friends in our Cub pack.

The me who put up a tent in ten minutes flat when everyone else didn't know where the poles went when we went on camp.

The me who can tell everyone which star they are looking at when we're sitting around the campfire.

The me who knows what type of bird is singing in the trees when we wake up in the morning.

The me who isn't useless at everything.

But I didn't think that was the me that anyone at school knew.

Then one day, about three weeks ago, something happened that changed my mind from me thinking everyone thought I was useless to knowing everyone knew that I wasn't.

My science teacher told the class that we were going to start looking at space and the sky.

I was so excited.

I knew stuff about space and the sky.

I was good at it.

Copyright © Naomi Richards and Julia Hague 2016

So every time the teacher asked a question about the night sky, I put my hand up.

And I got it right.

Every single time. Every question I got right.

The teacher stopped me after class and said how impressed she was with what I knew.

She said that she'd always known I was talented and I left the classroom walking on air.

I decided then that I should try more.

And that next week I should go and try out for the annual school play.

For the first time ever.

Because I don't know if I'm good at acting but I'd like to try and see.

And if I don't get picked then that's okay.

It won't be because they think I'm useless.

It will be because someone else might be better at acting than me.

Just like I'm better at naming stars and comets than everyone in my class.

I've realized that we can't all be talented at the same things.

But we do all have talents.

You just have to find out what and then show the rest of the world.

But you also have to realize that the rest of the world might just have noticed you were talented already.

Copyright © Naomi Richards and Julia Hague 2016

NOTES TO SUPPORT THE DISCUSSION

In Noah's story his friends always knew he was clever but Noah did not think so. Once he started to show that he knew lots about the stars and space he started to feel good about what he knew and his teacher was impressed. His friends probably were too.

Just like Noah we never know how good we are until we try. We never know how other people are going to respond to us when we share a part of ourselves that we think other people do not see. Most of the time we are pleasantly surprised and the response is good. People like what they see.

We need to share who we are so that others can learn from us and also see that we are not just one sided. We have lots of different interests and know lots of interesting things. Our thoughts can sometimes hold us back from trying, which is not helpful. If we can change those thoughts into more helpful ones we will be able to feel proud of what we know and want to try new things.

DISCUSSION QUESTIONS TO ASK THE CHILDREN

- What did you think of Noah's story?

- What do you think changed for Noah for him to start answering the questions on space?

- What different thoughts do you think he had?

- What do you think about second-guessing what other people think of you?

- How do you feel about showing off your talents? What is stopping you?

- Have you always wanted to try a new activity but haven't? If so, why not?

ACTIVITIES TO DO WITH THE CHILDREN

A DIFFERENT ENDING

Ask the children if Noah had not decided to put his hand up and get involved in the space lesson how do they think the story would have ended? Ask them to write another ending for the story.

TALENT SCOUTS

Ask the children to get into twos and design a poster encouraging people to participate in an activity they would like to take part in themselves. It should be something they do not already do or are not already are good at and should mention the type of skills they might learn by taking part.

PEN PALS

Get the children to write a letter to someone they have not met before and get them to share in the letter what they are great at, what they are good at and what they are not so good at.

DANGEROUS THINKING

Noah believed everyone thought he was useless and could not do anything well. If he was standing in front of the group what advice would they give him? How could they change his negative thoughts into more positive ones? Put the children into twos to share their thoughts and then ask them to share them with the group.

CIRCLES

Draw a large circle on the whiteboard and ask the children for general suggestions of skills/talents that they are good at and ones they are not good at but would like to be. Put the name of the skill/talent into the circle when it is called out. At the end see how many skills/talents are in there and how varied they are.

TONGUE-TIED AND...SCARED

(ABOUT BEING AFRAID TO SPEAK UP AND TELL FRIENDS WHAT YOU WANT)

SOPHIE'S STORY

EDUCATORS' NOTES

Suggested age for story – 9–11 years old

All children need to be able to stand up for themselves and not be bossed around, but not all children are able to do this easily. Some children find it difficult to say no to friends when they don't want to do something and therefore need to have the confidence to be able to assert themselves when they are with their peers. Being able to stand up for themselves will empower them and increase their self-esteem, which can have a knock-on effect in other areas of their lives.

This story looks at how children need to understand that not everyone in their group wants the same things as they do, and that they should never force friends to do something they don't want to do. They need to be more considerate and more accepting of other people's opinions and decisions.

All pre- and post-lesson exercises can be used for evaluation purposes if required.

LEARNING OUTCOMES

- Know what to say when standing up to your peers and have the confidence to do it.
- Do not feel pressured into doing something you don't want to do.
- Respect others' thoughts and feelings when they are different to your own.
- Understand the importance of speaking up.
- True friends will never make you do something you don't want to.

INTRODUCTION STATEMENT

Today's session is all about speaking up for yourself. There are times when we feel it is okay to stay in the background and let other people talk and make decisions for us, and there are times when we want to be more in control over what is happening in our lives. When you are quieter than your friends you can often get mistaken for being shy, however it can be that the friends around you talk more and talk louder so that you cannot be heard even if you did want to say something. Whether we are quiet or loud, we need to be able to stand up for ourselves when we don't like what our friends are doing to us or when we feel pressured to join in an activity that we don't want to take part in.

PRE- AND POST-LESSON EXERCISE

Before reading the story ask the children to write down a situation they have been in when they have not felt strong enough to say something to someone. How did they feel? After the story ask them to write down what they would have done instead.

Let's read Sophie's story. She used to get all tongue-tied and afraid to speak up in situations that she was not happy being in.

SOPHIE'S STORY

Everyone thinks I'm Quiet Mouse.

Small, brown haired and shy.

Walked over.

Trodden on.

Bossed around.

Timid.

But I'm not.

Well at least I don't feel like I am.

At least not in my head.

Or when I go over and over again what I'm going to say to Gillian and Priya in front of the mirror in my bedroom.

Then I'm Bold Mouse. Strong. Brave.

With a different voice.

But Bold Mouse's voice never comes out when I'm not in my bedroom.

Especially when I'm with my friends.

Bold Mouse is the brave me.

Standing in front of the mirror I'm rehearsing for the day I talk to them and tell them how I feel.

The day I say 'No.' In a Bold Mouse voice.

And when I'm pretending the words just flow. Easily.

And I look them straight in the eye and don't budge.

And I don't look down and end up mumbling. Like I always do.

Mumble so they don't hear what I say.

So they ignore what they can't hear and go on doing whatever it is they are doing.

Or sometimes I don't say anything at all. And the same thing happens.

But in my head that is worse. Not saying anything. I'd rather mumble.

Saying something so quietly that people don't hear, and you know they won't, is better than not saying something at all.

I sat on my bed the other day stroking Tommy and telling him all about it.

Copyright © Naomi Richards and Julia Hague 2016

He looked at me with the sort of look cats give you.

The 'I don't know why you are talking to me and being sad. But I love you' look.

I wish I felt like my friends loved me.

Actually I'd settle for 'liked me'.

I sort of wonder why I think they are my friends.

I tag along beside them.

Sometimes I feel like I'm that extra wheel on a bike.

Silent. Not squeaky or anything. So not an issue.

Not really necessary but okay to leave there.

Something you know…you forgot to take off.

It doesn't cause you any problems.

It's just there. Annoying maybe.

But you can't be bothered to get rid of it.

'Cos someday…maybe it might be useful. You know.'

That's how I feel I am with Gillian and Priya.

Because we never do what I want to do.

Or stop doing what I really, really don't want to do.

Like, for instance, hanging out after school on the way home in the park.

Waiting for the boys' school down the road to let the boys out.

And we sit on the bench in the park.

And we swing our legs and wait.

And wait.

And have magazines out.

So we can pretend like we don't care when groups of them walk past.

But Gillian and Priya do. Care, that is.

And they both put this light pink lip gloss on their lips and sometimes Gillian will make me put some on mine.

And I don't want to.

It doesn't feel right.

But I do it anyway.

Because it's easier than saying no.

And my heart always sinks.

I'm only just 11.

Copyright © Naomi Richards and Julia Hague 2016

I don't care what the boys think about me.

I don't want them to like me.

I actually don't want them to notice me.

So putting on pink lip gloss. Ugh.

So I end up gazing into my lap when the boys go past and call across at us.

So I can disappear into the bench.

And hide.

And not see them.

So they don't see me.

Or at least it feels like I've made it as hard as I can for them to see me.

Then Gillian and Priya call me an idiot, look at me with this disgusted look and link arms and march off out of the park with me trailing behind.

Me.

Feeling angry at myself for letting me be led into something I don't want to do.

And feeling frustrated that once again I look an idiot.

And perhaps more importantly I am sad that my voice let me down again.

And I scrape the pink lip gloss off my lips and throw the tissue in the park bin so Mum won't know.

Mum gets so frustrated with me.

When I'm late and I say that we've been at the park but I didn't really want to go she says that if Gillian and Priya are my real friends they would understand.

That friendship is about doing what both or all of you want. Not just what one side wants.

That I shouldn't be scared to tell them what I want or don't want.

That they would respect me more if I spoke up for myself.

I know Mum is right.

But it doesn't make it any easier.

But something happened today.

And I want to tell you about it.

I was walking home after another park episode.

There was a girl and her mum just going into the post office.

Quite a way down the road from me.

Copyright © Naomi Richards and Julia Hague 2016

Then the girl stopped and her mum went in and the girl waited.

She was younger than me.

Her face was pressed up against the glass of the shop window.

She'd put her school bag on the ground while she waited for her mum.

As I got nearer I saw two boys running across the road.

Towards the girl at the shop window.

They both stopped and she turned to talk to them.

She must have known them.

She was smiling.

Then one moved slightly and went behind her and pulled the bag from where it was resting next to her.

The boy with the bag turned and walked away.

Towards me.

The other boy went on talking to the girl.

I realized she hadn't noticed.

That her bag had gone.

That the other boy had distracted her.

Then the boy got closer.

To me.

He wasn't very big. Must have been at least six inches shorter than me.

My head started to tell my voice to speak up.

Quickly.

My voice tried.

It really did.

Then it faltered.

Like it always did.

And Quiet Mouse, all timid and shy, watched as the boy started to walk past me.

With the girl's bag.

And I wondered how I'd feel.

If my bag had been taken. And no one had done anything.

Then suddenly from nowhere, Bold Mouse took over.

I honestly don't know where she came from.

Honestly.

Copyright © Naomi Richards and Julia Hague 2016

But take over she did.

I reached across and put my arm in front of the boy to grab the bag back.

He stopped and looked at me.

Bold Mouse has a very bossy voice.

She was speaking loudly to the boy. She was strong. She sounded cross.

I heard her and wondered where she'd been hiding all these years.

While Bold Mouse was shouting at the boy and trying to explain that taking the girl's bag was wrong, the girl's mum ran up the street and caught up with the boy and me.

After making out it was all a joke, the boy handed the bag over to the mum and was told off by her in a voice even Bold Mouse couldn't copy.

When I got home, later than I had ever been, my mum was cross with me. I got the lecture that I always got, that I let people walk all over me and I should say no to my friends.

I didn't tell Mum what happened. Exactly. I just told her a boy had taken a girl's bag and the mum had caught him and I'd been there.

I didn't want her to interrogate me.

I felt different. Different because I'd finally released Bold Mouse and tomorrow would let her loose on Gillian and Priya.

Then I'd tell Mum everything. Because it would be such a fantastic story.

A story about a little quiet mouse who realized that by speaking up for someone else, she'd realized she could speak up for herself too.

That Quiet Mouse really was Bold Mouse in disguise and now the sky was the limit.

I put Bold Mouse to bed that night and hoped that Quiet Mouse would stay asleep in the morning and let Bold Mouse go to school instead.

Copyright © Naomi Richards and Julia Hague 2016

NOTES TO SUPPORT THE DISCUSSION

Sometimes we do get carried along with other people's plans and we forget how important it is for us not to go along with other people's wishes. We may want them to like us and be our friend and so we go with their flow and not our own agenda. Some of you may feel like this.

When we know we have to assert ourselves and feel confident, it can help when we stand tall – shoulders back – and rehearse what we are going to say to our friends in front of a mirror. What would you say to them and how do you think they would respond? It is important that we think about their response as that could change what we say to them. How would you feel if they reacted badly? Consider this before you speak to them so that you are prepared.

Remember that if someone insists that you do something you don't want to, especially when they know you don't want to, they are not really true friends. You have to consider if you really want to be with them at all.

DISCUSSION QUESTIONS TO ASK THE CHILDREN

- What do you feel about Sophie and her story?

- Do you think she could have done something different?

- Have you ever felt like a mouse? In what situations?

- What advice would you give to a friend who felt they were unable to stand up to another friend?

- How would you react to a friend who did not want to take part in something you wanted to?

ACTIVITIES TO DO WITH THE CHILDREN

THOUGHTS RELATED TO NOT SPEAKING UP

Ask the children to think about all those times when they did not speak up. How did it make them feel? Ask them to make a list of times when they did not speak up and next to it write down how it made them feel and then write a sentence about what they should have done instead.

SAYING 'NO'

Ask the children to get into twos. Ask them to think about the last time they said 'NO' to doing something they did not want to do. How did the other person respond? Did saying 'NO' feel good? Ask them to share their thoughts with their partner.

VALUES

Ask the children to consider what they believe in enough to say 'NO' to. Then ask them to jot down on separate post-its what these things are and then stick them on the wall for others to see. How many are the same? Group them together.

RESPECTING OTHERS

In keeping with the need to respect what other people want if they do not want to be a part of something, ask the children to spilt into groups and role play out what could be said between a friend who is trying to convince the other to do something and the other one standing up to them. At the end of the role play session, ask each group to report back on what kind of language was used and whether they felt that each of the friends respected each other.

I KNOW I CAN'T SO I WON'T

(ABOUT BEING FACED WITH SOMETHING
YOU THINK YOU CAN'T DO)

HARRY'S STORY

EDUCATORS' NOTES

Suggested age for story – 6–8 years old

There are times when children think they are not able to do something. That something could be skipping during the games lesson or spelling out a word in front of the class. It can be nerve-wracking for the child because they think they are not very good at that particular thing and therefore do not try to do it. What they don't know is if they had a little bit of belief and confidence they may just be able to do it and do it well or get it right.

This story should inspire children to feel more confident and raise their self-esteem. Once they see they can do something new they will be more likely to try that thing or something new again.

All pre- and post-lesson exercises can be used for evaluation purposes if required.

LEARNING OUTCOMES

- Believe in yourself.

- If you really want something you will succeed.

- Thinking of the feeling you will have, when you try something new.

- Inspire others to be brave too.

INTRODUCTION STATEMENT

It can be very scary when we have to try something for the very first time. We are not sure if we will do well at that thing or if people will laugh at us because we are not good at it and we may worry that something could happen to us in the process. These thoughts are all in our mind and can stop us from trying new things and having new experiences that we may love and be proud of.

We won't know if we are good at and enjoy something until we try, but first we need to change the negative 'I can't do this' thought into a 'I am going to have a go' thought. We can then get involved in lots of fun activities with our friends and not miss out.

PRE- AND POST-LESSON EXERCISE

What do the children think they are not very good at or worry that they are not going to be good at? Ask them before reading the story. After the story ask them if they would still worry about that thing.

Harry's friends could all swim but he was afraid to let go of the side in the pool. Let's find out if he ended up making it from one side of the pool to the other and, if so, how he did it.

HARRY'S STORY

I could hear James and Noah shouting to each other on the other side of the pool.

They were splashing around and enjoying the end of the swimming lesson.

They sounded like they were having so much fun.

Me, I wasn't.

My fingers were holding on tightly to the side of the pool.

The water was lapping around them.

My fingers were all wrinkly and white because I'd been holding on there for so long.

I looked across at the pile of orange floats and blue armbands and really wished I had one.

But I didn't.

Our swimming teacher, Miss Crowe, was talking to Natalie, a girl from my class just next to me.

She looked really scared.

She was also clinging to the side of the pool, nodding at the teacher.

Her bottom lip was trembling and she had tears in her eyes.

She looked across at me.

I knew she realized I felt the same fear.

Miss Crowe looked across at me

'Harry is going to show you how it's done.'

I heard my name and my stomach turned upside down.

Miss Crowe smiled at me and nodded.

It was her way of telling me to go.

To do the one thing I couldn't do.

Or thought I couldn't do.

Didn't want to do.

I heard more squeals from across the pool and saw Grace and Ella joining in with my friends, laughing.

They had all left their floats and armbands behind two weeks ago.

Miss Crowe cleared her throat loudly.

Copyright © Naomi Richards and Julia Hague 2016

'When you're ready, Harry,' she said encouragingly. 'Natalie's going to do it after you.'

I froze.

If I let go of the side and pushed off into the water I was on my own.

No swim bands, no float.

Nothing to stop me from sinking.

But Miss Crowe had shown me how to stay afloat last week.

How to swim a small distance.

I did it when she was in the water and right next to me.

But on my own I was terrified.

It was just that now there was no one to stop me from sinking.

At least I thought that.

I didn't realize that Miss Crowe could have reached me easily if I had started to sink.

My mind was just full of fear.

I couldn't think about anything else.

I saw Natalie's face.

Wide open. Expectant eyes.

I knew what she was thinking.

If I could do it, she could do it.

So I swallowed hard and turned around.

And then I pushed away from the side as hard as I could.

For Natalie.

So that she would do it after me.

And I didn't sink.

I kicked my legs and used my arms like Miss Crowe had shown me.

And I moved through the water so easily.

And it felt great.

As I got closer to my friends on the other side I heard Grace call my name and then the rest of my friends cheering.

I pulled up and let my toes touch the bottom of the pool when I reached my friends and knew that the smile on my face looked as big as it felt.

Copyright © Naomi Richards and Julia Hague 2016

I looked over to Natalie and I smiled and nodded.

Miss Crowe shouted 'Well done,' to me and then looked at Natalie.

As Natalie sailed across the pool too, Miss Crowe an arm's length away from her, I realized I'd finally swum across the pool because Natalie needed me to.

But actually I needed me to.

And I'd never felt so great in all my life.

Copyright © Naomi Richards and Julia Hague 2016

NOTES TO SUPPORT THE DISCUSSION

Harry was really brave to let go of the side and start swimming. He knew he had to give it a go and wanted Natalie not to be scared anymore and swim across the pool too. He realized that if he did it then she would have a go too. Harry could only do this if he did not think of all the things that could possibly go wrong and did think about what could go right.

He saw his friends at the other side of the pool and could see they were having so much fun that he wanted to be a part of that. So he went for it and let go of the side and kept swimming.

He only needed to do it once to prove he could swim and the next time he went swimming I imagine he would have not worried about it. His friends cheering him on would have made him feel wonderful and when we have the support of our friends it can help us try new things and be brave.

DISCUSSION QUESTIONS TO ASK THE CHILDREN

- What do you think of Harry and his story?

- What do you think was the main reason for Harry letting go of the side?

- What do you think Harry's friends were thinking about him?

- Have you ever been afraid of trying something?

- How did you make yourself try it?

- What is the best thing about trying something new?

- What could you do to feel less worried?

ACTIVITIES TO DO WITH THE CHILDREN

NEXT LESSON

Ask the children to write a letter to Harry before his next swimming lesson and remind him of what happened when he swam across the pool and how he felt, so he is looking forward to it.

STORY TIME

Get the children to write a story about a child who says they can't do something then tries it and sees they can. It needs to be about a page long.

BRAIN THOUGHTS

Ask the children to draw a picture of a brain and then inside the brain write lots of positive thoughts they could use instead of thinking 'I can't.'

TRYING SOMETHING NEW

Ask each child to write down on a post-it something new that they think they cannot do and put it up on the wall with their name on it. At the end of the year go back to the post-it and see if they have done that thing. Parents may need to get involved to help make it happen.

Part 4

PEER PRESSURE

STORY THIRTEEN

BOY TALK

(ABOUT NOT FEELING PRESSURIZED BY FRIENDS TO LIKE A BOY)

EMILY'S STORY

EDUCATORS' NOTES

Suggested age for story – 11 years old (end of Year 6)

It is not good when children feel under pressure to behave in a certain way because their friends are or to fit in with their peer group, especially when it does not feel right to them. Friends have a huge influence on children and not all of it is positive. Children need to do what they feel is right for them and stick by what they believe in. By going with those feelings they will be being true to themselves. When a child stays true to their values they become a stronger person and find it easier to resist peer pressure.

All pre- and post-lesson exercises can be used for evaluation purposes if required.

LEARNING OUTCOMES

- Do what you feel is right.

- Don't do what your friends are doing if you don't want to.

- There is no rush to grow up.

- Be true to what you believe.

INTRODUCTION STATEMENT

It is very easy to go with the flow when you are with your friends. You can get carried away with new activities that your peer group are doing and not really think too much about whether you actually want to be doing them or if they go against what you believe in. This is especially true when it is something that makes you feel grown-up.

We all grow up at different rates and some people are ready to have a boyfriend or girlfriend. Other children may not be interested at all and that is absolutely fine. We need to respect that we are all different. Some of you may like a boy or girl and be ready to go out for milkshakes with them. Others of you may just like being friends with a boy or a girl.

PRE- AND POST-LESSON EXERCISE

Ask the children to write down what they think of 11-year-olds liking girls or boys and meeting up like a kind of date before reading the story. After the story get them to write what they think of it again to see if their feelings have changed.

Let's read about Emily who liked boys but only as friends.

EMILY'S STORY

I like Max, I really do.

But I don't like him, if you get what I mean.

And I'm fed up that some of my friends keep pushing me to like him in that way.

I'm 11.

He's my really good friend.

We've known each other since we were five.

We've grown-up playing together in sandpits and swimming pools, been to each other's houses and played together with train sets, dolls' houses and computer games.

He's a boy but he's a friend and not a 'boyfriend' and there are some girls I know who just can't see the difference.

It's like if you are anywhere around a boy it has to be because you want to be girlfriend and boyfriend.

Seriously?

At 11? Or 12 or 13 or even older?

As far as I'm concerned you can have boys or girls as your friends.

I don't always agree with my mum but she's right, I'm going to have plenty of time when I'm older to have a boyfriend.

For the moment she says I should just enjoy having a good time with my friends – boys or girls.

I know Max would agree with me.

It feels like there's this pressure on girls to like boys in that way even when they're as young as me.

And it's coming from other girls, their friends.

Like it's the cool thing to do.

Like a club to be in.

If you can say you've got a boyfriend then you're super cool.

But that's the stupidest thing I've heard.

I want to be me.

Do things in my own time.

Copyright © Naomi Richards and Julia Hague 2016

When I want to.

I used to have this friend.

Amelia.

Amelia used to hang out with Max and me. When we were little.

She's a year older than both of us.

She's nearly 12.

She was in the class above us both at school but now goes to secondary school.

One day I was shopping with my mum and I saw Amelia walking along with a boy.

She didn't look like the happy Amelia I used to play with.

My mum tutted when she spotted them and steered me into a nearby shop.

'Why did you do that?' I protested, stretching my neck to see Amelia.

'Amelia's mum told me that she was pressurized into hanging around with that boy because other girls were hanging out with boys and she wanted to be like them. Her mum tells me she doesn't really like him at all.'

I was shocked.

Amelia had always seemed sensible.

Now here she was hanging out with a boy she didn't really like because the other girls thought she should.

I remembered the uncomfortable look on Amelia's face and so decided to phone her.

Amelia sounded really surprised to hear from me.

I told her that Max and I really missed her as a friend.

I asked her what school was like.

She said it was okay.

I told her I'd seen her with the boy.

I said she didn't look particularly happy.

To my surprise she didn't answer that.

Then she said that she really missed Max and me.

She asked if she could come and hang out with us at the weekend.

I said yes.

Copyright © Naomi Richards and Julia Hague 2016

That weekend Max and I listened to her tell us about how the other girls she had started to hang out with told her that a boy liked her and she should hang out with him.

She was too scared to say no, so she agreed so she could stay cool in their eyes.

Fit in.

She said the boy, Alfie, was okay.

Good fun to hang out with and just go to the mall with.

But she didn't like him. Not in that way. In fact, not in any way.

She wasn't ready to like boys in that way at all.

She just hadn't realized it.

She just went along with what other girls had told her she should do.

'You're an idiot, Amelia,' Max said, and I could tell he meant it.

'If you don't like hanging out with this Alfie, then don't. Don't do it because everyone tells you to. That's not fair on Alfie either. He might think you like him when you don't.'

Amelia nodded.

'I don't know how to get out of it now,' she said.

'Next time he asks you to hang out with him, say you're busy. You can always hang out with us,' I suggested hopefully. I missed Amelia. She was like my big sister.

'Yeah, hang out with us. There's a new boy at school – Sam. He hangs out with Em and me now. You'd like him. As a friend,' Max said.

Amelia hugged me. Then she hugged Max.

'I missed you guys,' she said again.

So Amelia started hanging out with us again. Sure, we were a year younger than she was, but she could be herself with us and she didn't have to like anyone or not like anyone.

No pressure.

Copyright © Naomi Richards and Julia Hague 2016

NOTES TO SUPPORT THE DISCUSSION

Amelia thought she was doing the right thing by going out with a boy because her friends also were. She may have felt the pressure to fit in with them and so went along with the plan to go to the mall with the boy. Once her old friend told her she looked uncomfortable with the boy, she recognized in herself that she was not ready for a boyfriend. She was happy having boys as friends and still doing silly things and having fun. She was not yet at the stage of her new friends and that was okay.

Some friends may encourage you to have a boyfriend or girlfriend when you are young or try to find out who you fancy. You don't have to share any information with them that you don't want to or do anything to please them. It is great to have boys or girls who are just friends and one great thing is that you get to learn more about the opposite sex.

DISCUSSION QUESTIONS TO ASK THE CHILDREN

- What did you think of Emily's story?

- What lesson did she learn from Amelia's situation?

- What else did you learn from the story?

- How do you feel about having friends who are boys/girls?

- Have you ever gone along with something to please your friends?

ACTIVITIES TO DO WITH THE CHILDREN

FRIENDSHIP WITH A BOY/GIRL

Get the children to write down all the advantages of having a friendship with a boy/girl. What is different in this friendship from one with someone who is the same sex as you?

CARTOONS

Ask the children to get into twos and create a cartoon to show what Amelia could have said to her friends who thought she should go out with the boy. Tell them to get Amelia to stand up for herself in the cartoon.

WHO FANCIES WHOM?

No one likes a gossip or wants you to invent that you like someone when you don't. Ask the children to role play in twos what they would say to someone who was making up this kind of stuff. Get them to discuss in their twos how it would make them feel.

LETTER TO A FRIEND

Ask the children to write a letter to a friend who is trying to persuade them to like a boy or a girl when they don't want to. The letter should explain to the child's friend how they feel about what their friend is trying to do.

STORY FOURTEEN

UNDER PRESSURE

(ABOUT BEING TRUE TO WHAT YOU FEEL AND KNOW)

WILLIAM'S STORY

EDUCATORS' NOTES

Suggested age for story – 7–9 years old

As children get older they need to understand what is wrong and what is right. They also need to learn the needs of their friends and know that when they are told something negative about a friend that it just isn't true. Children should know who to trust, who they can believe and that they need to stand up for their friends. It is also important that they ignore silly rumours. These are all life skills children need to have, and they need to be taught. If children can grasp these skills, their friendships will be stronger and this, in turn, will have a positive effect on their schoolwork and happiness.

All pre- and post-lesson exercises can be used for evaluation purposes if required.

LEARNING OUTCOMES

- Never listen to rumours or spread them yourself.

- Stand up for your friends when you know they have done nothing wrong.

- Telling the truth does not get you into as much trouble as lying.

- Some children need a bit of extra help and that's okay.

- Don't jump to conclusions.

INTRODUCTION STATEMENT

It is important to stand up for your friends and to know that if someone says something untrue about them you can put them straight. Spreading rumours is unkind. It is also important that you think before you say something unkind or say things that are not true about another person. No one wants to be around people like that.

We also need to be aware and have a greater understanding of other people's needs and their learning style. For instance, some people find it easier to use a computer in lessons rather than writing with a pen and others need to have pictures to learn rather than words. We should not think that those using means of learning other than pen and paper are getting it easier than us. They aren't. They just need a different way to learn.

PRE- AND POST-LESSON EXERCISE

Before you read the story ask the children to write out a short piece about when they saw someone doing something that was different to everyone else and assumed it was wrong. After the story ask them to write down whether they would now act differently.

There are lots of lessons to be learnt in William's story about learning and friendship. Let's hear what happened to him and his friend.

WILLIAM'S STORY

Jack and Nathan – two Year 6 boys – cornered me one lunch break last week.

They told me that my best friend Max had cheated in a test we'd had that morning and would be in big trouble.

Really? I could not believe it.

But they said they had seen him doing it through the window of the classroom.

And they were going to tell on him.

'That's rubbish,' I said angrily.

I could feel myself going red in the face. And I felt a bit scared. They were big boys and I would never have dared say anything to them before.

But Max was my best friend.

'Yeah, well just wait and see,' Jack said laughing.

They gloated as they said it and one of them shoved me as he pushed past.

As if the shove made what they said even more realistic.

I stared after them.

Max had been my best friend since reception.

Max always told the truth. He always told his parents if he'd done anything wrong. Always. But he never really got into trouble because he hated doing anything bad and he never lied.

He said that it was always better to confess and risk getting told off.

He said that denying doing something hurt more than telling.

So when Jack and Nathan told me he had cheated, I knew it wasn't true.

Couldn't be true.

In my heart.

I wondered if they had made it all up.

To make me think bad things about Max.

But they didn't really know us.

For the rest of the lunch break I started to feel bad that I had even listened to them.

Especially when I knew it was a load of rubbish.

Copyright © Naomi Richards and Julia Hague 2016

Two girls from our class came and sat at my table in the dining room, Clara and Hannah.

They told me that they'd heard rumours about Max cheating. That 'he obviously wasn't such a goodie-goodie as he always made himself out to be'.

I told them what a load of rubbish it was.

That Max couldn't cheat. 'He wouldn't even think of it.'

That what they were saying was nasty and wrong.

They shrugged as if I was lying and walked off.

I remembered what Max always said to me, that you should never lie and always tell the truth.

I had told the truth.

I knew it was right.

I would tell Max what they said when he came back from his extra lunchtime lesson with Mrs Falconer, the dyslexia tutor.

Then he could make sure that the lies being told about him were stopped.

So I walked towards our classroom.

Then I saw Jack and Nathan.

They were coming out of the head teacher, Mr Salter's office. With their class teacher.

I could just make out what she was saying to them as they walked with her down the corridor.

Their faces bright red.

'I hope that this will teach you not to spread nasty rumours about someone again,' the teacher was saying. She sounded cross. 'Detention at 3.30. Your parents will be told.'

My heart leapt.

I hoped it was about Max.

I knew it had to be.

Why else would they be coming out of Mr Salter's office if it wasn't?

And then I saw Max.

He was coming out of Mr Salter's office too. After the others.

He spotted me and ran over.

'You'll never guess what…' he said grinning.

Copyright © Naomi Richards and Julia Hague 2016

'That stupid pair, Jack and Nathan from Year 6, told Mr Salter that they saw me cheating this morning in our test. They said they saw me with a piece of paper on the desk which I was reading from. How stupid are they?' Max laughed.

Max saw my puzzled face. I didn't think anyone was allowed to have notes to read from in tests.

'Don't you get it?' he said, 'I'm having my test questions written out in a different format because of my dyslexia and they thought I was cheating because everyone else was looking at the questions from the whiteboard. So they told on me.'

I laughed with Max.

Max was always right.

Doing something wrong never works out. Jack and Nathan found out that afternoon.

But do you know what the best feeling of all was?

Knowing that I hadn't doubted what I knew about my friend, even when others said they knew better.

Copyright © Naomi Richards and Julia Hague 2016

NOTES TO SUPPORT THE DISCUSSION

This story addresses several issues. The first one is that it's important to stick up for friends and believe in them especially when those around you don't. The second is no good ever comes of rumour spreading and usually the person spreading the rumour will get into trouble in the end. The third one is using different ways of learning is very common. It's just that we don't often see it happening in front of us. We need to be aware of others managing work in different ways and accept this is the way it is for some children.

Max handled the situation really well and so did William. William stood up for his friend and never doubted him. He knew exactly what his friend was like and believed in him. That's what friends do.

Max was confident in how he was managing his work and was not fazed by the older boys trying to get him into trouble, and he did not feel that he needed to tell everyone about the extra help he was getting. You don't need to go around telling everyone everything about yourself. It is your business not theirs. For example, if you go to a booster lesson, no one needs to know why. Only you need to and if you want you can tell your friends. Friends can support you if you need a little extra help with your schoolwork and if they are real friends they will stand up for you if others are not so supportive.

DISCUSSION QUESTIONS TO ASK THE CHILDREN

- What did you think of the story?

- What was the main thing you learnt from it?

- How well do you think William dealt with the older children?

- What did you think of Max?

- What would you have thought if you had seen Max's paper on his desk in the test?

- Do you think the older children did the right thing by saying he was cheating?

- What do you do when you hear something nasty being said about someone?

ACTIVITIES TO DO WITH THE CHILDREN

APOLOGIZE!

Ask the children to put themselves in the older boys' shoes and get them to write a letter of apology to Max for saying things that were not true.

ALL STAND UP

Get the children to stand up in a circle and one by one share what they could do to stand up for their friends. What would they say or do? Can each person think of a different way?

MANAGING WORK

Thinking about the story, ask the children to imagine different ways in which schoolwork and tests can be managed if someone is having difficulties and get them to display their ideas in poster format.

RESEARCH

Get the children in groups to research dyslexia and find out as many facts as they can about it. They can make a fact file in their groups.

Part 5

BEING UNIQUE

WISH UPON A STAR

(ABOUT BEING YOURSELF – YOU'RE FAR MORE INTERESTING)

HOLLY'S STORY

EDUCATORS' NOTES

Suggested age for story – 10–11 years old

Children need to understand that their idols and the role models they see on TV and in magazines are not always as they seem. They are often told to act and look a certain way and this is how they earn their money. When they are away from a camera or a TV lens they are no different to how ordinary people are. Children need to realize this – that everyone is the same and that they should not put other people on a pedestal. When children realize that celebrities they have never met are the same as them, they will be more accepting of themselves – especially their flaws.

All pre- and post-lesson exercises can be used for evaluation purposes if required.

LEARNING OUTCOMES

- People may not be what they appear to be when viewed in the media.

- Celebrities are ordinary people.

- We should never want to be anyone else.

- To be a role model you need to model kind, considerate behaviour.

INTRODUCTION STATEMENT

We all have days when we are unhappy with the way we look. We want to hide until our hair goes the way we want it or when we don't have a spot on our face. Unfortunately, we do have to face the world and go to school or out with mum or dad. Life does not go on hold until we have a good hair day or lovely looking skin. It does not help though when we see celebrities looking great in magazines. We can often think to ourselves, 'I would love to look like her,' and wonder how they look so good all the time. How are they so beautiful, popular, perfect, wonderful etc.? The answer is, they're not!

Celebrities have their good days and their bad days. They are normal. We should not think of them as being better than us. Yes, they may have great talent, but so do we. We are just not in newspapers and magazines like they are. The only person we should want to be is ourselves, so when you find yourself obsessed with a celeb think about what they would be like if you met them. They may not seem what we expect in terms of their personality or looks.

PRE- AND POST-LESSON EXERCISE

Ask the children to write a sentence about what a role model should be before the story. After the story ask them if what they wrote is the same as what they would write now.

Let's read Holly's story. Holly was a 'wannabe'. She was in awe of a celebrity. She put her on a pedestal until she saw the other side of her favourite celebrity – the not-so-good side. It made her question what a role model should be and appreciate who she was.

HOLLY'S STORY

It happened again last week.

That feeling.

That whatever I wear.

However I put my hair up.

No matter whether I think the shoes I'm wearing are pretty cool.

However much I scrub my face or brush my teeth.

I'm never going to look like HER.

And then I cried.

And got angry.

And sat in my room hugging my cushion and staring at HER posters.

Because I wanted more than anything to look like HER. And so be like HER.

Then Mum came upstairs and knocked on my door and asked me what was wrong.

And I told her to go away.

But she came in anyway because she knew.

I had the magazine on the bed in front of me.

Spread out with HER picture across the middle.

Seeing my tearstained face, Mum sat down.

'You're beautiful just the way you are,' she said.

'But SHE's so pretty! She's more beautiful than me,' I shouted.

'Holly, look at her. She has had her hair and make up done by a hairdresser and beautician and her clothes were picked especially for the photo shoot. They have probably photoshopped her teeth so they look white and airbrushed her body a bit.'

'I've seen HER on the television and SHE looks the same,' I protested. 'I want to be pretty like HER.'

'Holly, if you met her in the flesh. Standing in front of you as she opened her bedroom door she'd be just like you. With no make up and no hairdresser, standing in her pyjamas.'

'If I looked like HER my life would be perfect.' I went on sniffling.

Copyright © Naomi Richards and Julia Hague 2016

'Would it? Being pretty isn't everything sweetheart. Life is more than being good looking or pretty. Besides, you're gorgeous anyway.'

I know Mum means well but I'm nearly 11 and I feel like I'm in a race. To be perfect and beautiful. When you're little it doesn't matter what you look like as everyone thinks you are cute anyway. But now I am older I'm heading into the unknown when strange things are starting to happen to my body and I want everything to be perfect.

Mum asked me why I felt this way.

'Because if you're perfect and pretty and you have white teeth and a lovely smile, then everyone likes you and wants to be like you,' I said. 'You're kind of like a role model. I want to be a role model and have everyone think I'm amazing.'

Mum asked me if I honestly thought that being a role model only came with being pretty.

I said 'yes', that was what I thought. All the girls thought like that at school too. Everyone wanted to be the pretty one.

I had pushed my magazine in front of her and pointed at HER.

'SHE's got everything, Mum. Everything. Surely you want me to be the same and be liked by everyone? Wouldn't that be fantastic?'

I felt excitement rise as I said it.

'I'd love you to just look at yourself and see how beautiful YOU are Holly. Being in a magazine, being a pop star, a model or an actress doesn't automatically mean you are perfect or liked for that matter.'

I couldn't answer her. I just knew that looking pretty was the way to get liked and the way to be.

'Honestly Holly. If everyone looked the same it would be a sad and boring world. Beauty isn't about hair, make up or clothes. It's about what is inside you. So concentrate on being the loveliest person inside. Then you'll be surprised at what happens.'

Mum always said the same thing. But it didn't make any difference.

Then yesterday my world changed. You could say it turned topsy-turvy. Overnight.

And boy did it hurt.

Poppy, my best friend rang the house phone.

'Did you see the news?' She sounded out of breath and tearful.

Copyright © Naomi Richards and Julia Hague 2016

'No, why? I just got up,' I answered.

'SHE didn't turn up at HER concert and everyone waited for hours and hours for HER. Then SHE turned up at the last minute, didn't apologize to the fans and SHE ended up pushing someone because they got in HER way.'

My heart sank. I couldn't believe what I was hearing. SHE had always seemed so nice in interviews. So genuine.

'But Poppy, SHE's so lovely,' I managed to say in a splutter.

'They're saying SHE's not! Switch on the TV. One of the fans filmed it on their phone. Everyone's saying it's the real HER that's come out. They're being really horrible about HER.' Poppy spluttered something about being utterly devastated about the whole thing and then put the phone down.

I ran downstairs to the kitchen where Mum and Dad were sitting having breakfast.

The TV was blaring away in the corner.

'Your lovely pop star's been a bit of a let-down, love,' Dad said, as I slipped onto a chair at the table and Mum thrust a bowl of cornflakes in front of me.

'Can I see what they said?' I replied, pretending not to care but my heart was thumping.

Dad flicked to the catch-up bit and up came the piece on HER.

I stared at the screen. SHE didn't look like HER. SHE looked tired. Angry. Out of control. HER hair was messy and HER eyes were dark. SHE didn't look like HER at all. I saw HER push the person away and say really bad things to them. They had bleeped the sounds out. But you could see SHE said them.

Mum slipped in next to me and put an arm around my shoulders.

'You know, Holly, she's just human. Like all of us. She should have apologized to the people at the concert. And she certainly shouldn't have pushed anyone.'

I left the table and went back up to my room. I knew Mum and Dad would be giving each other knowing looks but I didn't look back as I climbed the stairs.

I sat on my bed for what seemed like ages.

Copyright © Naomi Richards and Julia Hague 2016

And then I stood up and looked in the mirror and stared hard at my eyes. They stared back.

What I saw was a clean, make up free, fresh face.

A face that had no agenda. No knowledge of what I was going to be.

A blank canvas, my mum always said.

I then glanced at the poster on the wall and saw the smiling face, white teeth and perfect clothes staring back at me. Surface beauty. Underneath she was like all of us. Normal. Made mistakes.

But we had one big difference. She and I.

She had been a role model to hundreds of thousands of girls. Me included.

She had made those girls like her. Want to be her. Not want to be themselves.

I am not a role model to anyone. Yet.

I might one day have people like me.

But I never want those who like me not to want to be themselves.

Because in the end being ourselves is far, far better than trying to be someone else.

Besides, we don't really know what those people are like. Inside.

We do know what we are inside.

I didn't take her poster down. I forgave her. She was human.

Pretty, yes. But human. I liked her more for making a mistake.

I just hoped that in the days to come she would apologize for it.

Then I would know that you can be pretty and nice but actually the being pretty part isn't everything. The nice part is.

Copyright © Naomi Richards and Julia Hague 2016

NOTES TO SUPPORT THE DISCUSSION

We know it is what is inside that counts and it really shocked Holly to find out that her role model was not as polite as she thought. She had a temper and thought it was okay to be late for her concert. We know that is disrespectful.

There are always people we will look up to because they inspire us and we want to be like them in one way or another. Whoever they are we need to admire them for the right reasons. Perhaps they have done something miraculous and outstanding for the world. Perhaps they have raised lots of money for charity or they have created something we use daily. Perhaps they stand up for something we care about or have an opinion on. If they haven't then why are you looking up to them?

DISCUSSION QUESTIONS TO ASK THE CHILDREN

- How do you feel about Holly and her story?

- What lessons did she learn about celebrities?

- What did she learn about herself?

- Do you think it is important to be pretty?

- What would you say the most important quality is to have?

- How do you feel about the way you look?

- Would you want to look like someone else?

ACTIVITIES TO DO WITH THE CHILDREN

LOOKS ARE NOT IMPORTANT

Ask the children to think about what is important if looks are not. Get them to write down a list of ten things that are more important than being told you are pretty/beautiful/good looking.

WHOM DO YOU ADMIRE?

Ask the children to think of someone who they admire and research them on the internet. Get them to write down ten facts about them and why they think they are special to them and then turn those facts into a poster using pictures and colour.

LOOK CLOSER TO HOME

Ask the children to divide into pairs. Get them to write down one thing they like about their partner and then pass it to them to make them feel good.

BEING A ROLE MODEL

As individuals, get the children to think about what they would want to be known for if they were role models. Ask them to write a paragraph about themselves and give themselves a superhero name too.

STORY SIXTEEN

STYLE STATEMENT

(ABOUT DRESSING HOW YOU WANT TO EVEN IF IT IS DIFFERENT)

SARAH'S STORY

EDUCATORS' NOTES

Suggested age for story – 9–11 years old

When a child has their own style it shows creativity and a sense of being comfortable in their own skin and not wanting to follow the crowd. It allows them to show others their own taste and gives other people a hint of who they are. This topic area of dressing how you want to will help children to think more freely about the individuality of those around them and accept that we are all different in our tastes. It should encourage them to be less judgemental and see beyond the way someone dresses.

We want to encourage children to do this, as it is part of their development and finding out who they are and what they like. They will be more comfortable in their clothes and therefore display themselves in a confident manner. This will influence the way they interact with others in a positive way.

All pre- and post-lesson exercises can be used for evaluation purposes if required.

LEARNING OUTCOMES

- Children being more accepting of how others dress.
- Learning not to judge a person on what they are wearing.
- Be confident in what you wear and how you look.

- Style comes in many different forms.

- Everyone is unique.

INTRODUCTION STATEMENT

There is so much pressure these days to look a certain way. Girls and boys are very aware of how others dress and can often decide if they are going to be friends with someone because of the way they look. Children want to fit in yet want to have their own individual style. What can children do though when they want to dress comfortably yet want to fit in? Sadly, to some degree, there is still stereotyping when it comes to clothes. Most magazines still show girls wearing light colours in dresses or feminine clothes and boys in darker colours. Whereas in reality many girls like to wear dark colours, even black as they get older and many boys like to wear lighter colours. The media also focus on what is in fashion and will dedicate pages to photos of models in very feminine clothes.

We need to encourage children to be themselves, dress in what they feel comfortable in and not feel the need to conform. If a girl wants to wear trousers all the time that should be fine. The same goes for a boy who wants to wear pastels or have a ponytail. Children need to accept that other children want to be individual too.

PRE- AND POST-LESSON EXERCISE

Get the children to write down a sentence about how important they think it is to dress a certain way and how they think it would affect friendships. After the story ask the children how they feel about the story and see if their thoughts have changed.

Let's meet Sarah, who doesn't want to dress like everyone else. She has her own style, embraces her uniqueness and knows what she likes. Isn't that a good way to be?

SARAH'S STORY

I'm really fed up with seeing girls in magazines always looking like…well, girls.

I don't look like a typical girl.

It's that simple.

I don't like girlie clothes.

Oh and…

I NEVER wear dresses. EVER.

I like jeans and a t-shirt or jeans and a sweater and trainers.

I don't do pink or purple either. I really, really like black. Sometimes green but mainly black.

You see black is a colour which no one notices. Black kind of hides you. It wraps itself around you and lets you get on with just being you. Hidden inside it.

It's the greatest colour ever invented.

Oh and no, not trainers with stupid flashing lights on them or multi-coloured laces. Just trainers.

You might ask me what I'm doing looking at magazines that I obviously don't like.

You see I'm secretly wishing that one day I'll see a girl who looks like me staring back from the pages of the magazines.

It's only a small wish. Honestly.

I mean, like, it doesn't run my life or anything.

But I'm curious.

Because I feel like sometimes I must be the only girl in the whole world who dresses like me.

Which is kind of fine actually.

But when I turn the pages of girls' magazines in the newsagents, I open each page just hoping – slightly – to see another girl with short hair and black t-shirt and jeans. So then I'll know that the magazine and all the people out there in the world reading it are celebrating what it is to be ME.

And I'll get to see what it looks like on another girl.

I know I'm different.

But that's okay. And I'm happy with that.

Copyright © Naomi Richards and Julia Hague 2016

Different is good.

One day someone said something at school. Something rude about the way I looked.

That's when I first realized I was different.

It didn't bother me. It just made me realize what they saw.

At home I never knew I was anything other than me.

I played games with my brothers and loved fighting with wooden swords and pretending the stairs lead up to the top of the castle.

And some days I'd be a ninja and creep around the house.

I loved my life.

So when this girl tried teasing me at school it didn't work.

I wasn't sure what she wanted me to do.

Change because she thought I didn't look like her?

Be like her because she said so?

It wasn't going to work.

But that's okay. I quite like looking like a boy but not actually being one.

I like the fact that in a way I'll always look different to most girls.

And I can dress how I want to.

Because I want to.

It's fun.

I don't get asked to be involved in the games that the girls play, which is great because I don't want to play girlie games. Instead the boys let me join in with them because I'm good at playing their games. So I can be a ninja or a knight or an alien and run around with them and be loud and be ME.

And when I shop for clothes with Mum she is really cool and lets me choose what I want and doesn't push me into buying girlie clothes.

I don't feel that my whole dressing life is dictated by what other girls think about what is cool or fashionable or whatever stupid rules that someone somewhere who doesn't know me has made up that girls have to wear.

I'm me.

I'm a girl.

Me.

Sarah.

Ninja-loving, alien-fighting, individual me.

Copyright © Naomi Richards and Julia Hague 2016

NOTES TO SUPPORT THE DISCUSSION

Sarah had the right attitude. She embraced her individuality and made it work for her. She could play with the boys and was not bothered about what the girls said. She liked being who she was and wanted to be comfortable dressing in her way.

Not everyone will have the same taste as you in clothes. Some people dress for comfort and choose their own clothes. Other children are dressed by their mum or dad and so have less choice about how they look. It is important to find your own style and wear what makes you feel comfortable so that you can concentrate on enjoying growing up.

Do not worry about what others think. Wearing what you want shows you are an individual and unique. If anyone does call you names maybe they are just jealous that you look good.

DISCUSSION QUESTIONS TO ASK THE CHILDREN

- What do you think of Sarah and her attitude towards being herself?

- Do you think she did the right thing?

- Have you ever felt like you did not fit in, in the way you looked? How did you overcome those thoughts?

- How important do you think it is to fit in?

ACTIVITIES TO DO WITH THE CHILDREN

RAPPING IT OUT

Get the children to divide into groups and compose a rap that describes their group in the style of each child's dress preferences. If they feel brave, ask one or two of the group to share the rap with the rest of the children.

MAKING A COLLAGE

Ask the children to make a collage of themselves using magazines and their own drawings to demonstrate the way they like to dress.

BEING UNIQUE IN YOUR STYLE

Who do the children admire for their style and why? Get them to write a couple of paragraphs about this person. They can also illustrate their piece of work.

DON'T JUDGE

Get the children to write a letter to a clothes store highlighting the fact that they should not stereotype and asking them to make a wider variation of clothes for both boys and girls that incorporate colour, design and cut.

JUST ME

(ABOUT BEING POPULAR BUT WANTING TO BE YOURSELF AND NOT LIVE UP TO WHAT OTHERS THINK YOU ARE)

OLIVER'S STORY

EDUCATORS' NOTES

Suggested age for story – 10–11 years old

Many children want to be the popular child – the one whom everyone adores and wants to be with. They see the advantages of having lots of friends and it is something they want too. There are some children though who are popular and don't like it. They do not like to be followed around or be the centre of attention. They do not see what all the fuss is about and they would rather be seen as a regular child who is not put on a pedestal.

This story illustrates that it is important for you to just be yourself – the good and the bad. And if others think you are perfect, to put them straight. When you do, you will be far happier than having the pressure from friends to be something you aren't. People will still like you and if you are popular it will be by default. You will not feel like a fraud.

All pre- and post-lesson exercises can be used for evaluation purposes if required.

LEARNING OUTCOMES

- Be yourself around all your friends – not just your best friend.

- Don't feel pressurized to be the perfect person everyone wants you to be.

- It might appear great to be popular but there can be disadvantages.

- Real friends accept everything about one another.

- If it's not an all-through school, then secondary school can bring a new start.

INTRODUCTION STATEMENT

Some of us are happy to blend into the background and not be noticed. Other children like to be the centre of attention and be the 'popular' person in their class or their school. Some children try to be popular whereas for others it just happens. There are positives to being popular but there are also negatives and that all depends on the kind of person you are. There can also be some pressure on you to behave a certain way when you know you have younger children or your peers looking up to you.

This story is all about the pressure to be someone that others want you to be even when you know you are not.

PRE- AND POST-LESSON EXERCISE

Ask the children to write down how they would feel if they were the popular child in their class or their school before reading the story. After reading the story ask them again to write down their thoughts about the same question. How different are they?

Oliver was the most popular boy in his class. People at school thought he was Mr Perfect. All he wanted was for them to see that he wasn't – he was just like them. He has faults too. Here is Oliver's story.

OLIVER'S STORY

My name is Oliver. Ollie sometimes. Depending on who I'm with.

I'm nearly 11.

I'm really good at football. Really good at drama. First in the class in science and I'm popular.

Sounds like I'm boasting and full of myself.

But I'm telling you all of this because I'm not. Full of myself, that is.

I'm just me.

Oliver.

And it's true that I am good at football and drama.

There's nothing wrong with saying that.

There's nothing wrong with being honest about something you're good at.

As long as you don't boast.

Because that sounds pretty lame when you do.

I am top in science too. I find it easy. I love it.

Can't change that. Wouldn't want to.

See I'd like to do something in science when I grow up.

I ace maths. I haven't failed a test in class ever in any subject.

I can't help that.

But the popular bit…

I am. But I don't want to be.

That's the thing I'd like to change.

Crazy, huh?

Yeah.

I have to live up to this kind of image that the other kids have of me.

The kid they want to be.

The kid they want to be with. Hang out with. All the time. Go everywhere I go.

Because they think I'm something.

Something I don't feel I am.

They've heaped all this stuff onto their image of me that now it's become a truth.

Copyright © Naomi Richards and Julia Hague 2016

In their minds.

Not mine.

And I don't know how to be the real me anymore when I'm around the others.

Because I'm afraid that maybe they won't understand or like the real me if I am.

Does that make sense?

Sure I can be myself at home.

With my brother who's older than me. And my two sisters who are younger than me.

And my parents.

I can goof around and make mistakes. Which I do by the way.

I can giggle at silly TV and sit with my sisters and play games that are way younger than me because they love it and actually so do I.

I can go over and hug my mum when I go upstairs to bed while she's watching TV with my brother. I can do it because there's no one around to think that's uncool.

Hugging your mum when you're ten.

Because they probably all do it too.

But of course it's uncool for anyone to know.

So lame.

I can lose to my older brother when we play football in the garden.

It doesn't happen often because I'm on the team and he never has been, but it does happen.

You see, I am a normal kid really.

I mess up.

I get things wrong.

I worry about stuff.

To those who think I'm the person they want to be, the perfect person with the perfect life, they wouldn't get that.

You might be thinking that if I showed them the real me and they didn't like me and so I wasn't popular anymore, that would be a win. Yeah?

Copyright © Naomi Richards and Julia Hague 2016

But letting other kids into that side of my life and seeing the me who messes up and maybe isn't the kid they thought I was, is too scary at the moment.

My dad told me that sometimes it's good for kids to see that everyone is the same. That no one is that special that they never mess up or goof around. That everyone is really deep down like everyone else.

He's right.

But it's still difficult to get out of something that has been following you around for years.

But I have a plan.

I'm going to secondary school in September.

I figured out that when I go there I can start again.

No one will think I'm Mr Perfect, so I won't have to be.

My really good friend Tom is the only friend who I let see the real me. The goofy, messing-up me.

He knows how I feel and it's going to be cool that he is going to the new school with me. Sure, there's two other kids going there but no one is going to listen to them.

My brother told me something that made me laugh.

He said that I'm going to be changing from 'a big fish in a small pond to a small fish in a big pond' when I change schools.

That's great!

I'm going to be quite happy being a little tiny fish swimming around in the big pond out of everyone's way and let some other person be the big fish.

And only I'll know what that feels like.

And I'll be the one not wanting to be like that kid.

★ Copyright © Naomi Richards and Julia Hague 2016

NOTES TO SUPPORT THE DISCUSSION

Oliver was not happy being popular as he thought he was not being who he really was when he was around his friends. He felt only his best friend and family knew the kind of person he was despite him wanting the children at his school to see his bad side as well as his good side.

He wanted this to change and so was looking forward to a fresh start at secondary school where he would be a small fish in a big pond and not everyone would take notice of him and follow him around. Of course, there will be people who want to be around him and he hopes those people will see him for what he is – warts and all!

DISCUSSION QUESTIONS TO ASK THE CHILDREN

- How did Oliver feel? Was it justified?

- How do you think you would feel?

- What lesson did you learn from the story?

- How important do you think it is to be popular?

- Is there anyone who you think is popular? Why do you say that?

ACTIVITIES TO DO WITH THE CHILDREN

QUALITIES

What makes someone popular? Ask the children to list as many qualities as they can, then write next to them if they possess any of these qualities. Also ask them to write down the qualities they think they have that don't necessarily make them popular but they like having.

USING POPULARITY TO YOUR ADVANTAGE

Get the children to choose someone in the public eye who uses their popularity to their advantage and design a poster about them.

FRESH START (FOR PRIMARY SCHOOLS)

Irrespective of being popular and having lots of friends or not very popular with not many friends, what would a fresh start when they go to secondary school mean to the children? Get them to write a letter to themselves about what they hope to achieve friendship-wise.

CHANGES (FOR ALL-THROUGH SCHOOLS)

Get the children to think about their next move into the senior school and new children joining the school. What would this mean to them? Ask them to write a letter to themselves about what they hope to achieve friendship-wise.

MAKE A STAND

(ABOUT KNOWING YOU ARE RIGHT AND ASSERTING YOURSELF)

BRANDON'S STORY

EDUCATORS' NOTES

Suggested age for story – 10–11 years old

Standing up for yourself and what you believe in is so important to do. If children don't, then they are doing a discredit to themselves and letting others take control of something they believe is wrong. Children can often go along with a group of friends because they are not 'that bad' and overlook it when they are mean to other children. They do this to be accepted and be a part of something. However, there can be a time when a child questions who their friends are. This can happen when a new child comes into the school and they see their friends behave in an unkind manner to the new child. Then it may be time to make a stand and move away from the friendship group and join together with people who are kind and do not call people names.

We need to teach children the right way to behave and to know that it is wrong to stay with a group of friends who do not like them to have friends outside of their group. Friends are not possessions. None of their friends has the right to tell them whom they can or cannot be friends with. We need to give children the confidence to walk away. If they can do this it will make them stronger people.

All pre- and post-lesson exercises can be used for evaluation purposes if required.

LEARNING OUTCOMES

- Stand up for what you believe in.

- Include others and know how to treat them.

- Friends are not possessions.

- Don't let any of your other friends tell you who you can or cannot be friends with.

INTRODUCTION STATEMENT

It feels great to feel part of a friendship group. You belong to something and are included in arrangements and playtime activities. For some of you, though, you may have friends who are not always nice to you or to other people and so being part of that group may not be the best thing for you. What your group says or how they act may not be what you believe in. For example, calling people names is wrong, and so is trying to stop the people in your group talking to other friends. Most of you know that this is not the right way to treat others. If you feel your friends are not very kind you need to decide whether you want to stay friends with them, tell them it is wrong and that you don't want to be a part of it anymore. That takes lots of guts but it can be done. Brandon did it. His story is coming next.

PRE- AND POST-LESSON EXERCISE

Ask the children what they would do if their friends were calling other people names before you read the children the story. After the story ask them if they would do anything differently.

Now let's read Brandon's story.

BRANDON'S STORY

I don't know what made me do it that day.

I just know that from that day forward I changed.

Changed how I felt about myself.

In a better way.

And changed how I felt about others.

And it was all because of a boy who I didn't know.

Well, I didn't know at the time.

But I do now.

Because now we're best friends.

But before that things had been different.

I always used to hang out with the same group.

There were five of us.

We'd been a group since Year 2.

Most of the time we had a laugh. We had fun and would talk about football and music.

But sometimes they'd be really mean about other children in the school – even to their face.

Sometimes they would make them cry.

They were never kind to new people either and would definitely not let them hang around with us.

I knew it wasn't right but I liked my friends and I felt comfortable being a part of the group.

We were in our last year at school and about to move to secondary school.

And about a month ago a new boy joined our class.

It was pretty unusual to get a new child join so late in the school year.

Most of our class were too busy to notice the new boy. Some thought there was no point getting to know him because they were changing schools. But I liked the look of him and I felt kind of sorry for him too.

A new school was scary for anyone, especially when you joined right in the middle of a term or worse still at the end of the school year.

Copyright © Naomi Richards and Julia Hague 2016

And then to have everyone get on with their lives and ignore you.

I imagined what it would feel like.

Probably lonely and scary.

I wondered if I could get to know him outside of our group.

So he'd just be my friend.

It was the last school year after all.

My crowd probably wouldn't notice.

So a few days after he'd joined the class I asked my mum if it was okay to invite him over after school.

Of course Mum said yes.

His name was Aleem. He seemed surprised when I asked him to come to my house but his parents said it was okay.

He came over the following day.

Aleem and I got on really well.

He was fun and had moved down to our area from the north of the country and had lots of stories about his old school and friends.

For the first time in a while I realized I was laughing a lot.

Mum commented when Aleem was collected that she hadn't seen me have as much fun for ages.

And so far my group hadn't realized he and I had become friends.

I'd kept it kind of a secret.

At the end of the next week Aleem and I decided to go to the park to kick a ball around after school.

My usual group had invited me to go and play with them but I said no, that I had something else to do.

I should have known they would have been curious.

So after we'd been kicking a ball around for a while I heard my friends' voices drifting across the park in my direction. They'd followed us.

Then I realized that they were shouting really nasty things at Aleem.

Then calling at me to join in with them.

Aleem stood there and stared at them.

He looked shocked.

Then he looked at me.

Copyright © Naomi Richards and Julia Hague 2016

And my friends looked at me.

Everyone was waiting for a reaction.

From me.

Whose side would I be on?

As I watched my friends being mean I realized what I must have looked like when I was with them.

Being nasty to people.

And it didn't look nice.

I also knew that the things my friends were saying were really, really wrong.

Mean and ugly.

That they had always been wrong.

That I didn't want to be a part of it.

Anymore.

So I did something I should have done a long time ago.

I stood up for what I believed was the right thing to do.

I moved in front of Aleem and shouted back.

I told them that what they were doing was wrong.

That it had always been wrong.

That I was out of their group.

Forever.

I looked at each of their faces.

My friends.

And I knew that they couldn't be that anymore.

Because they weren't like me anymore.

Or I wasn't like them.

That I needed to be true to what I was.

And it wasn't a bully.

And it wasn't a mean person who thought nasty things about people.

It was a person who was prepared to stand up for what they believed in.

Were there consequences?

Sure.

They called me horrible names and they've been pretty mean to me for the last two weeks.

Copyright © Naomi Richards and Julia Hague 2016

Dad said that they'll grow tired of being mean to me.

My mum told me a long time ago that we have a duty to make our corner of the world a great place to be.

And that includes how we treat the people in our lives and who we meet.

She's right.

My mum and dad really like Aleem.

So do I.

And I like something I haven't really liked for a long time – I really like me.

Copyright © Naomi Richards and Julia Hague 2016

NOTES TO SUPPORT THE DISCUSSION

Brandon knew what was right when it came to treating his friends but it was only when the new boy came into the class that he realised he did not want to be a part of his friendship group anymore. Seeing them call Aleem names highlighted for Brandon what his friends were really like and he knew he wanted to leave his old friends behind. He evaluated what he believed in and took a stand.

He enjoyed Aleem's friendship and by spending time with him realized he was having more fun than when he was with his old friends. He also began to like himself again because he was being a good person – kind, honest and true to himself.

It was difficult at first for Brandon to leave the group but he stuck the name calling out. It is important to stick something out. Whatever changes you make in life there is a period of adjustment and some of it is not nice. During this time we need to be strong and know that it will get better. You have to think about what is right for you and the end result.

DISCUSSION QUESTIONS TO ASK THE CHILDREN

- How do you feel about the story?

- Do you think Brandon did the right thing?

- What do you think of Brandon's original friends? Do you have friends like that?

- What do you think Brandon's friends thought when he made a stand?

- What would you have done in his situation?

- If Aleem had not started at the school do you think Brandon would have stayed with his friends?

- How do you think Aleem felt when Brandon stood up for him?

ACTIVITIES TO DO WITH THE CHILDREN

CARTOONS

Get the children to do a cartoon strip of Brandon's situation adding in speech bubbles showing the conversations from the start to the finish of the story.

FRIENDSHIP BELIEFS

Get the children into groups to make ten types of playing cards where each card shows how children should treat each other. They can be as creative as they like so long as it is clear what the quality is.

PLAY IT OUT

With the children in groups of four get them to role play a different ending to the story so that on the playing field Brandon's friends don't call Aleem names. What happens instead?

SMALL CORNER

Remind the children of what Brandon's mum told him – that we all have a duty to make our corner of the world a better place to be. Ask the children what things they could do in their school/family/community to make things better for people. Discuss other things people could do.

Part 6

FRIENDSHIP

BFFS – WHERE'S MINE?

(ABOUT NEEDING A BEST FRIEND)

BREE'S STORY

EDUCATORS' NOTES

Suggested age for story – 7–9 years old

Children need to know that having a best friend is not important or necessary. What is important is that they are social, get along with most of their peers and have a friendship group of people they can enjoy being with. Once they stop chasing and searching for a best friend forever (BFF) they will get to enjoy the friendships they do have and not worry about a BFF. They will have more fun and be more relaxed if they have this mindset.

A lot of friendship disagreements amongst children are about one friend being possessive of another. Children need to understand that friends are not possessions and that everyone must have the freedom of having more than one good friend if they choose to.

All pre- and post-lesson exercises can be used for evaluation purposes if required.

LEARNING OUTCOMES

- Children do not need one special friend to make them happy.

- To see the value in having many good friendships.

- Accept that some people just end up having a BFF and some don't.

- No one person can be everything to a friend.

- A BFF is not a 'must-have' accessory.

- Friends are not possessions.

INTRODUCTION STATEMENT

Today's topic is all about friendships and having best friends. Some children like to have a best friend – someone special – as it makes them feel safe and secure. Other children like to spread their wings and don't like to be tied down to one person. It all depends on the type of person you are and how confident you feel in yourself. If you feel good about yourself and have a healthy self-esteem then you may be happy to have lots of different types of friends and not one close friend.

We should not feel jealous of others who have a best friend. We should see it as a good thing that they have someone they can rely on and trust. We should always let our friends have other friends if they choose to, just as we can have more than one friend.

PRE- AND POST-LESSON EXERCISE

Before the story, ask the children if they think it is important to have a best friend and get them to write the reasons for their answer down. Ask them also to rate out of ten how important it is to them to have a best friend. After the story, ask them the same question again, get them to write it down and see if their answer is different.

I am going to share Bree's story. Bree felt that she was missing out on not having a best friend and could not understand why she didn't. Her story does not have an ending so perhaps we can create one for her.

BREE'S STORY

Everyone's got one. Everyone.

Even Sasha, the mousiest girl in school, hangs out with Nikki. Arm in arm, like two glued together penguins, they walk around all day, giggling and laughing and being...BFFs.

Then there's Misha. She and Clara sit every break time together with their heads touching, whispering on the bench in the playground.

There's a rule isn't there when it comes to BFFs?

Everyone's got to have one.

Someone to tell your secrets to.

Someone to laugh with at stupid things.

Someone to hang out with at weekends.

Someone who sticks up for you.

Someone who you stick up for.

Someone who is yours.

But here I am.

No BFF for me.

I've got friends of course. A whole group.

It's just that there isn't one of them who is like...well, mine I guess.

You know, like only hangs out with me.

That special friend.

The one.

So where did I go wrong?

What am I doing that means no one wants to be attached only to me?

I had this chat with my big sister the other day.

Caroline is 16 and she has this really interesting take on the whole BFF thing.

We sat.

Me swinging my legs on the end of the bed talking away as I always do.

Her gazing at the TV and half listening to me.

Copyright © Naomi Richards and Julia Hague 2016

So I grabbed the remote, hit the mute button and leapt over to the other side of the room.

Caroline protested loudly and reached for it.

'Not until you answer my question,' I said.

I held the remote behind my back and gave her the look.

She sighed and turned over grabbing the pillow to lean against.

'What question was it again?'

'What am I doing wrong? Why doesn't anyone want to be my best friend?'

Caroline gave me the 'oh my god not that again' look.

'That's two questions,' she replied. 'What's so important about having a best friend anyway?'

'Everyone needs one. I need one,' I grumbled.

'No you don't. You've got loads of friends,' my sister said.

'Not one to call my own.'

'Look Bree, friendship isn't about owning someone. Even if you have a best friend, they can still be best friends with someone else as well.'

'No they can't. When you have a best friend you do stuff with them and only them,' I argued.

'No you don't. There isn't some rule that says you can only have one best friend,' Caroline retorted.

Caroline then lost interest and attacked me to get the remote back.

Must say I didn't resist much.

I wasn't getting anywhere with Caroline. I still didn't know why I wasn't attracting that 'bestie'.

I had a talk with my brother too.

Yes. Shock horror. My brother.

He's my twin.

He gives good advice.

When he's not being a complete pain.

'Why do you want to hang out with just one person?' he said.

'Because a best friend is forever. You never have to worry about other people. You've got this person to be mates with and even if people are horrid you don't have to care. Because you've got this person who is there for you, who likes you for being you.'

Copyright © Naomi Richards and Julia Hague 2016

He tried to advise me. 'You've got loads of friends and you're always out or on the phone with them. If you only had one friend you wouldn't hang out with the others. And it's not the end of the world if you don't have a best friend, Bree.'

He made plain sense to other people I'm sure, but not me.

I sighed and looked away. I muttered under my breath.

'It is to me.'

I'm not sure I'll ever know why I feel the way I do.

Like I'm missing out on something big in my life.

Because everyone seems to have a BFF.

Everywhere I look. On cards in the shops, on the TV, in magazines – they talk about the BFF.

So everyone has one.

Except me.

And one day maybe someone, someday, will be able to tell me why.

Why I haven't got one and why I care so much.

Until then. I'll just keep waiting. And wishing.

Copyright © Naomi Richards and Julia Hague 2016

NOTES TO SUPPORT THE DISCUSSION

A BFF is not necessarily going to make you feel wonderful, safe and secure. Having a BFF in theory is great in terms of having someone to rely on and have fun with but no one person can be everything to you. It is not possible for them to have all the qualities we want in a person.

If you don't have a best friend and want one, if it is meant to happen, it will. Just be friendly with everyone and be a good friend and the BFF may appear. And if they don't, remember that it is good to have lots of special friends who you can go to depending on how you feel. There can be friends you want to be with when you are happy, sad or excited or when you have a secret to share.

DISCUSSION QUESTIONS TO ASK THE CHILDREN

- Do you understand how Bree feels?

- Is there anything she can do if she wants to have a best friend?

- What would you say to her if she was one of your friends and complaining she needed a BFF?

- How important is it to have a BFF?

- Do you have a BFF or lots of friends?

- If you do have a BFF, what do you do when they are not at school? Who do you then spend your break times with?

- How do you think the story should end?

ACTIVITIES TO DO WITH THE CHILDREN

HELPING SOMEONE LIKE BREE

Ask the children to get into twos and discuss what they would say to Bree to help her think differently about having a best friend. Get them to practise role playing one of the conversations they would have with Bree and then show the rest of the group.

WRITING A LIST

Get the children to do a list of the pros and cons of having a best friend and then do the same for having lots of friends.

WHAT HAPPENS NEXT?

Ask the children to write a paragraph to show how the story ends, since there is no ending.

WHO HAS A BFF?

Give out a piece of paper to everyone in the group and ask them to write down their friends' names and alongside each name if that person has a BFF. They will see that not everyone does.

WHO IS IN YOUR LIFE?

Ask the children to make a list of the friends they have in their life and then add a column at the side that shows one thing that makes them a good friend or special to them. What qualities do they like in them?

PLEASE LET IT BE ME...
PLEASE LET IT BE ME...

(ABOUT SURVIVING BEING THE LAST TO BE PICKED)

KATE'S STORY

EDUCATORS' NOTES

Suggested age for story – 7–11 years old

Friendships are not easy to navigate and they get tested in many different ways. We can think someone is a good friend but they turn out not to be. They can often appear loyal and trustworthy but when it comes down to standing up for you or saying they will do something for you, they don't. They can really let you down.

This story will teach children the importance of being resilient and accepting that not every friend will treat them as they would treat others. In fact, not everyone will treat them well. Some will even go back on their word.

Resilience is an important life skill that all children need to get on in the world. If they can acquire this skill they will be able to overcome obstacles and difficult situations.

All pre- and post-lesson exercises can be used for evaluation purposes if required.

LEARNING OUTCOMES

- Friends don't always do what they are going to say.

- Sometimes we have to let go of a friendship.

- Our friendship values are not always the same as our friends'.

- Friends can let you down.

- Good things can come from not very nice situations.

INTRODUCTION STATEMENT

We are going to talk about friendships today and how you can be friends with someone for ages but then a new girl or boy can join the class or a good friend can leave the school and your friendships can change. Sometimes you have to move away from a friendship because that person has upset you in some way and sometimes we don't feel that we have anything in common with a friend anymore. We have to know when to say goodbye to a friendship or pull away a bit from someone. It is not easy to do and requires strength and confidence. By the end of today's session I hope you all feel that you are confident enough to make friendship changes now or in the future.

PRE- AND POST-LESSON EXERCISE

Before reading the story, ask the children to write down what they would do if a good friend let them down. At the end of the story ask them what they would do now. The growth in ideas should indicate the session was a success.

There is an unwritten code between two friends of how they should treat each other and in the story I am going to read you, that code has been broken. It is a sad story with a happy ending and it reminds us that sometimes our friends are not who we thought they were.

KATE'S STORY

OMG that hurt. Really hurt. Like physically or something.

Seriously. Who does that?

I felt like I was never going to be friends with her again. I thought she was my best friend. Some best friend.

I had been so happy when Chloe was told at the beginning of the PE lesson that she was going to be one of the team captains.

We'd both dreamed of being allowed to be a captain for a lesson. Me, because I couldn't imagine what it would be like to actually get to choose my team mates and Chloe just wanted it. And today…finally I would get to be chosen for a team instead of left till last like some unwanted sweet wrapper stuck on someone's trainer.

For her first choice Chloe chose Hannah. I felt hurt. She hadn't called my name. But then I kind of accepted it. After all Hannah's the best at netball. Chloe would be an idiot not to pick her. She's tall. She scores. I got that.

But then, as Chloe waited for Jess, the other team captain, to choose her first team member, that voice came into my head.

I thought I was Chloe's favourite. I'd have chosen Chloe first. I'd have made a statement to the whole of the class. She's my friend and look I'm showing you all.

I told myself off again.

Hannah's the best. It made sense. Of course she picked her first.

Now it was Chloe's turn to pick again.

Chloe chose Rebecca.

I tried to catch Chloe's eye. But she looked away. I know it was on purpose.

I should have known this was going to happen. That her being captain was not going to mean she would choose me. She hadn't even smiled at me when she'd been told she was captain back in the changing rooms. My best friend had ignored me!

See, I hate netball. I'm no good at it. I'm short. I can't throw to save my life and my feet kind of get caught over one another when I'm going for the ball and I end up in some kind of messed up heap on the court.

Copyright © Naomi Richards and Julia Hague 2016

I know it's not my thing. I have lots of other things but it's not one of them. But we didn't care I was that way. Chloe and me. We just liked each other.

Or so I thought.

I felt like I was going to throw up. I think I went bright red. Of course I don't know because thankfully no one was looking at me. They were all eagerly staring at the two captains wanting to be picked. I could almost hear them saying, 'Me! Me! Let it be me!'

I knew it wasn't any good looking hopefully at Jess, the other captain. She hated me. Made my life a misery most of the time. The chance of her picking me was about…oh let's see…zero.

And then, as always, I was left to last. And Jess had to take me on her side. Chloe had taken Bethany, the new girl, and I just stood there. Abandoned.

By my so-called best friend.

So we played. Chloe's team won, by the way. Jess dug me hard with her elbow as we left the netball court. Blaming me for her team not winning. Of course.

I glanced across at Chloe. To give her a disappointed, hurt look.

But Chloe wasn't looking in my direction. She was arm in arm with Hannah, laughing together.

Hannah. The girl Chloe had always pretended not to like. The most popular girl in our year because she was good at everything and Chloe had always said to me that she was too sporty for her liking. That she preferred me. Now she was arm in arm with Hannah?

I looked around at lunch break. The lunch hall was full. I wasn't used to not having Chloe to sit with. I panicked for a minute.

'Kate!' Bethany's voice drifted across to me. 'Come and sit here.'

I sat down and started to unwrap my sandwich.

'Glad it was you, not me, who got picked last this time,' Bethany said through mouthfuls.

I didn't know Bethany well. Hadn't paid her much attention.

'It's always either you or me,' she continued. 'I was surprised Chloe didn't pick you and picked me. Being your friend and all.'

'Yeah, well…' I couldn't finish off. My throat hurt.

Copyright © Naomi Richards and Julia Hague 2016

'Always thought you and Chloe were tight. No one ever gets a chance to get in between you two.'

I remember chewing my sandwich slowly. I hadn't thought about anyone else really. Other than Chloe.

'I'm no good at sport. That's all,' I said. It sounded really stupid as I said it. Friendship wasn't about being good at something. Well, not in my eyes anyway.

'Me neither. But I don't think it was very nice of her anyway,' Bethany said and I caught her shrugging her shoulders as she ate her lunch.

I looked across at what Bethany was reading. A dragon was on the front cover. And a girl with a sword. Cool.

As I got up from the bench I knew that morning I'd lost something.

Then I looked across towards Bethany and realized that maybe I'd gained something.

Copyright © Naomi Richards and Julia Hague 2016

NOTES TO SUPPORT THE DISCUSSION

The best thing that seems to have come from this horrible situation was Bethany and the possibility that the two girls could become friends. Sometimes good things do come out of bad situations and when we feel sad about how a friend has treated us we need to think about the other people we know who we could play with and get to know. People we did not really know before.

We need to see a friendship failing as an opportunity to talk to other people and find out more about them. You never know, you may have more in common with them than your previous friends. To spread yourself wider you could even sit with different people at lunchtime and get to know them and then choose who you would like to hang out with.

In this story maybe Bethany has other friends she could introduce Kate to. There is always a possibility that a friend will introduce you to more people.

DISCUSSION QUESTIONS TO ASK THE CHILDREN

- What do you think the story is about?

- What do you think about Chloe?

- Do you think Chloe and Kate can still be friends?

- What would you do if you found yourself in that situation?

- Would you have been forgiving?

- How do you think the story will end?

ACTIVITIES TO DO WITH THE CHILDREN

QUALITIES GOOD FRIENDS HAVE

This story questions what makes a good friend. Ask the children to each list on a sheet of paper ten qualities a friend should have.

THE PERFECT FRIEND

Draw a figure of a child on the whiteboard and ask the children to contribute single words that describe what a perfect friend should be. Write the words up next to the drawing of the child.

DEALING WITH THESE HURT FEELINGS

Ask the children to imagine they are Kate. Ask them to write a letter to Chloe about how they are feeling and what they would have done differently if they had been in her shoes.

ROLE PLAY

As a group, role play picking teams and what you think about when you pick teams. Do the children go for the ones best at that activity or their friends? Ask the children to give a reason why when they pick someone, but they must keep it positive and friendly.

TRIBES

(ABOUT BELONGING TO A GROUP)

LOGAN'S STORY

EDUCATORS' NOTES

Suggested age for story – 10–11 years old

Children are very aware of the friendship groups at school and know who belongs in which group and who is friendly with whom. They are also aware of who does not fit in. Whether a person has a group or not, children need to be welcoming to their peers and make them feel that they belong.

All pre- and post-lesson exercises can be used for evaluation purposes if required.

LEARNING OUTCOMES

- Don't fall into the first group of friends when you go to secondary school.

- Keep an open mind when it comes to making new friends.

- Don't change to fit in with a friendship group.

- No one is better than anyone else.

- Be friendly with everyone.

- Don't be scared to change friendship groups.

INTRODUCTION STATEMENT

We all want to belong – to feel accepted by a group of people, by friends. It makes us feel happy, safe and included. When we belong it means people like us. Some children find their friends quickly, some think they have found them and then discover they are not the right friends for them and other children take their time to make good friends as they want to make sure they are the right tribe for them.

PRE- AND POST-LESSON EXERCISE

Ask the children to write down two circumstances that would make them feel like changing their current friendship group before reading the story. After the story ask them to write down whether those two circumstances would still make them feel like changing groups, and if not, what had changed their mind.

Logan was part of a group of friends that he did not respect and he was unhappy. He had to make a big decision. Should he stay or should he go? Let's read Logan's story.

LOGAN'S STORY

I know a lot of you think that being in the cool gang is really the only thing that matters.

That strutting your stuff like one of those tigers you see at the zoo is really so important and that being in a gang of other strutting tigers is like…well, you've got it all, haven't you?

But you know something? Being in the cool group is not everything.

I bet you are thinking, how can he say that? He's wrong. The cool people have it all.

Well, I do know. And the cool people don't have it all.

I know because once upon a time I was one of those strutting tigers. And I honestly believed my world was perfect. That life couldn't get any better. That I was better. Somehow. Than the people not in the cool gang.

But it turned out I was wrong.

You see I never intended that I would end up as a strutting anything. Now I feel bad about calling the group I was with tigers. Not for them. For tigers. Because they're actually really noble animals and they strut around because that's their thing. And our group certainly wasn't noble.

With the group I ended up in, they were trying to make everyone else feel bad about themselves. Like, 'Look at me I'm special and you're not.' 'You can't be in a gang of tigers because you're never gonna be good enough.' So when I first started in my new school and this boy came up to me and was friendly to me, I was excited and…almost relieved. I had an instant friend.

It's hard enough moving schools without any of your friends.

Hard to walk into that classroom on the first day and feel like a hundred eyes are boring into you like hot lasers. Judging you. Looking you up and down and a hundred silent whispers of 'yeah he looks okay' or 'nope, don't like him'. Making up their minds in a moment's glance at you. When they don't really know you.

But that's life I guess. We all look at people and take an instant liking to them or not. It's not right. But it happens.

So yeah, I admit, I welcomed the friendly chat. And the welcome smile.

Copyright © Naomi Richards and Julia Hague 2016

At that time I didn't know he was one of the cool group. It took me a couple of weeks to realize that.

The other boys he hung out with seemed okay too. Nothing special but I began to notice that when we walked past other kids they would turn or move away or pretend to be having a conversation.

I didn't like some of what they said about the other kids.

At first I ignored it and didn't join in. But after a while I found myself being carried along with their conversation and I could hear things coming out of my mouth about other kids, which I honestly hated myself for. Especially as I didn't know the kids they were talking about. I said the things just to be accepted. To be cool.

The boys in my group accepted me more. Often I'd walk with them in a group past other kids in the school and I stupidly felt good about myself because I belonged.

To this group.

And for some reason I felt it mattered.

And I thought I could see from other kids' faces when we passed them that they thought we were so important. That our group was special and so exclusive. And how lucky was I to be a part of it.

Or how stupid. I had persuaded myself that the other kids thought I was important. That my group was important. More important than any group they were in.

Actually, in reality, they were scared of us. Scared that our tongues would lash down nasty things on them. But instead I kidded myself that they were desperately wanting to be one of us, because we were so cool.

In fact, if they did ever want to be one of us, it was because then they wouldn't be teased or bullied. Not because they liked us.

So yeah. I'd managed to get into a group that everyone was terrified of.

Really cool. Not.

But it's hard to leave something that you feel you belong to, especially because in my heart I guessed if I walked away from them I wouldn't belong anymore and I'd be alone. There would be no going back.

Not with this group. If you got out, you stayed out.

Copyright © Naomi Richards and Julia Hague 2016

And then you could become one of the kids they bullied or teased.

Then I realized that I didn't know anything about anyone else in my class.

I'd been so wrapped up with the cool gang that I'd ignored everyone else.

So how could I find a group to belong to? Or even just one friend?

I couldn't bear the thought of being friendless. I deserved to be shunned by the rest of the kids. True. But really? Everyone needs to feel like they belong to something.

So one day I sat down with Dad and told him everything.

He raised an eyebrow when I told him how cruel the group had been to everyone and I gulped when I told him I'd been a part of it.

My mum and dad are always honest with me. Sometimes I think they're too honest. But on the whole they're always right.

Dad told me to join a club or an activity outside school hours that none of the cool gang would find remotely interesting because it didn't involve strutting around and pretending they were better than everyone else. Like the astronomy club or the film club. Two things I was really interested in.

He told me to break away from the group gradually. For my own sanity.

He said to make friends in the new clubs and then start telling the group I couldn't go with them wherever they were going.

Good advice I thought. So I tried it.

Did it work?

Well, sort of.

Actually I don't know for sure yet.

I joined the film club. It meets once a month. I've been twice.

At first the kids in the film club looked at me in horror when I walked in the first time. One of the group they all feared. But I stuck it out. Said some nice things to a couple of them and left. The next time I actually talked to the same two kids about the film.

Next time I might even get invited to go to the cinema with them. Who knows? I heard a few of them making arrangements at the last meeting and looking at me warily.

Copyright © Naomi Richards and Julia Hague 2016

But so far no invitation.

I don't blame them. I would do the same thing. But I'm hopeful.

And I've started not going to so many places with my old group. Yeah, they ragged me about the film club but I didn't back down.

I've also stopped joining in saying horrid things about or to others in the class.

It might take months for me to get away from them.

But I have to do it.

Because we can change tribes. We're not born into the groups of friends we choose to be with. We choose our friends. If we know in our heart that the group we are with is wrong, then we owe it to ourselves to be with people who like what we like and act like we do.

Mum told me to always think of friends as reflections. Our own.

You need to look in the mirror and see the reflection looking back at you and know that it's right.

So yeah, be a tiger if you want to be, but sometimes a giraffe, or a lama or a zebra is just as nice. You've just got to find out where you fit and make it happen.

Copyright © Naomi Richards and Julia Hague 2016

NOTES TO SUPPORT THE DISCUSSION

What a powerful story. Logan was really brave to make a decision to leave the old group and then slowly move away from them. It can be really difficult to do but if you find yourself in a similar situation don't worry. Do it gradually like Logan. It will take time to fit into another tribe but persevere. The most important part is that you recognize which tribe that is. You can do this by talking to other people, finding out who has similar interests to you and starting to get to know them better. It is also important for you to just be yourself and let them see the real you.

Friendships change a lot in primary and secondary school. You will eventually find your tribe – some good friends you can have fun with. There is no rush so take your time and chat to lots of different people when you start secondary school. If you find a group that you have something in common with then spend more time with them and see how the friendship develops naturally.

DISCUSSION QUESTIONS TO ASK THE CHILDREN

- What do you think about Logan?

- Do you think he did the right thing? What else could he have done?

- Would you have done the same or would you have stayed with the group?

- Why do you think the group behaved like that?

- Have you changed your behaviour to fit in with a group? What change did you make and how did you feel about yourself becoming that person?

ACTIVITIES TO DO WITH THE CHILDREN

PUT YOURSELF IN LOGAN'S SHOES

Get the children into groups of four and ask them to share ideas of what they would have done if they were Logan and then role play it out.

WHO ARE YOU?

Ask the children to think about who they are as individuals and make a list of all the things they like to do so that they can find like-minded individuals.

WHAT DOES A GOOD FRIEND LOOK LIKE?

Get the children to write down what qualities they look for in a friend. Ask them to get creative – draw a person and write the qualities inside the body of their drawing. Explain that if they look for these qualities in potential friends they are more likely to find their tribe.

BEING CONSIDERATE WHEN MOVING FRIENDSHIP GROUPS

Arrange the children into small groups to discuss the best way to move friendship groups and then share those ideas with the group. What would they say to the old group, if anything at all? How could they subtly move to another group?

ODD ONE OUT

(ABOUT NOT BEING INVITED TO A PARTY WHEN ALL YOUR FRIENDS ARE)

DANIEL'S STORY

EDUCATORS' NOTES

Suggested age for story – 6–8 years old

Children need to understand that they are not going to be invited to every social event that takes place out of school. There will be times when the whole class is not invited to a party as a child has to choose a few friends to celebrate their birthday with. It can be upsetting when you aren't one of those chosen children, but it is something that children have to accept.

Not getting an invite may at first be a shock but it can get the child to think of a logical reason why they did not receive one. A common logical reason may be that they are not as friendly with that child as other children.

Understanding why they did not receive an invite will encourage greater thinking skills and resilience. A resilient child will bounce back after rejection and this is a life skill all children need to have.

All pre- and post-lesson exercises can be used for evaluation purposes if required.

LEARNING OUTCOMES

- You cannot be invited to every party.
- Some children are only allowed to invite a few friends.
- We all view friends differently.

- You may think someone is your good friend but they don't see you as a good friend.

- There is always a good reason why you did not get invited.

INTRODUCTION STATEMENT

We all see friends differently. Some people we call our best friends may not say we are their best friends. Some children may say they get on great with a friend but the other person may say they fight all the time. So when it comes to organizing a party it can be easy or difficult for a child to make a decision about who to invite.

Many parties will be restricted on numbers because of the cost. When your mum says you can only have five friends, who would you choose? It is not easy as you do not want to upset anyone. The same goes for other people inviting you. Often we can feel left out because we have not been invited and we think we should have been.

PRE- AND POST-LESSON EXERCISE

What do the children think about not being invited to a party? What is their first thought? Get them to write it down before reading the story. After the story get them to write down their new thought about not being invited to a party.

Here is Daniel's story about a party invite he expected but never received.

DANIEL'S STORY

There was a giant dinosaur bouncy castle.

There were burgers and fries and fizzy drinks.

There were balloons and party bags.

There was music.

There were games.

There was Dylan and George, Alex and Thomas.

Even Lily, Ruby and Amy went.

But there wasn't me.

Ethan's seventh birthday party.

Last Saturday.

And I didn't get invited.

I went out to the shops with my mum and my big sister instead.

We went past Ethan's house in the car on our way to the shops.

We had to.

He lives at the end of our road.

The balloons were tied to the front door.

Mum drove straight past and onto the road that led to the centre of town.

My sister poked me and pointed at Ethan's house.

My sister can be very mean.

Mum told her off.

I looked away.

I didn't cry.

I'd cried too much last week.

See when Ethan came into school with the party invites and started handing them out I got excited.

I wasn't friends with him but I did live down the road and our mums had coffee together a lot.

So I was expecting to be invited.

When I didn't get an invite I remember going to sit at my desk in the classroom.

Copyright © Naomi Richards and Julia Hague 2016

I put my head down and glanced at my reading book pretending to read.

I could feel the tears trying to come out.

My cheeks felt hot and red.

And I had a lump in my throat so big it made me swallow hard.

It hurt.

A hot salty tear rolled down my cheek and I rubbed it away roughly.

I couldn't let anyone see me cry.

Amy came and sat down next to me.

'Sorry you're not going to Ethan's party, Daniel.'

'It's okay. I didn't want to go anyway, I'm busy that day,' I said. I was lying.

Mum has always told me not to lie. But I couldn't help it.

'My mum says it's not nice to hand out party invitations in front of people when you're not inviting everyone in the class,' Amy said.

'Yeah, well. I don't care. I couldn't have gone anyway.'

This time I hoped it wasn't a lie.

When I got home I asked Mum if we could go out. I told her about Ethan's party.

She put her arms around me and hugged me.

'You're not really friends with Ethan are you love? It's hard to invite everyone to a party. It's expensive you know.'

'Yeah but all my other friends are going.'

'Maybe they're better friends with Ethan than you are.'

Mum promised that we would go out that day so that I could be away from the road when the party was going on.

So we went to the shopping centre and I did have fun there. On our way home I glanced at Ethan's house but it was quiet and the party had finished.

When we got home Mum sat me down.

'Listen love, if I told you that you could have a party and that you could invite ten friends from school, would you invite Ethan?'

I thought about it. Started counting my friends on my fingers. I had about 12 names.

'There's 12, not ten. Can't I invite all of them?'

Copyright © Naomi Richards and Julia Hague 2016

'If I told you it was too expensive to invite more than ten and you had to choose, who would you pick?'

I thought about it again. More counting on my fingers. It was so hard.

'Not Ethan,' I said.

'Because you weren't invited to his party?' Mum asked.

'No. Because he's not really my friend. I have ten friends I like more,' I replied.

Then I smiled and realized that mum was proving a point.

Ethan wasn't my friend. We never played together.

Sure, he did play with some of my friends but not me.

So it made sense that he wouldn't invite me if he had to choose.

On Monday back at school I asked Amy if she had enjoyed the party and she said it was great.

'My birthday is next month, Daniel. Hope you won't be busy when I'm having my party because you're on the invitation list.'

I grinned.

I wasn't the odd one out. I was exactly where I was supposed to be. With my real friends.

Copyright © Naomi Richards and Julia Hague 2016

NOTES TO SUPPORT THE DISCUSSION

Daniel really expected to receive an invite to Ethan's birthday party and felt left out that he hadn't. He thought he would have been because their mums were friends. However, it was only when he thought about who he would have invited to his own party that he realized Ethan would not have been on his list.

We cannot expect to be invited to every party and even if we have invited someone to ours we should not expect an invite back. There will be many times when we aren't and it may make us upset. It may not make sense to us that we did not receive an invite back but we need to tell ourselves it is okay and there must be a good reason for it.

We cannot change anything about the situation apart from what we do. Crying and getting upset will not change someone's mind about inviting us.

DISCUSSION QUESTIONS TO ASK THE CHILDREN

- How did Daniel feel about not being invited?

- Could he have felt differently?

- What advice would you give Daniel next time?

- Would you have lied about why you could not go anyway?

- How do you feel when someone hands out invites in front of you?

- How difficult do you find it when you can only invite a few friends to your party?

ACTIVITIES TO DO WITH THE CHILDREN

CHOOSING YOUR INVITES

How do you choose who you will invite to your party? Ask the children to make a list of how they choose those people. Are they their best friends that they play most with or is there another reason?

GET CREATIVE

Put the children into twos and get them to design an invite for their perfect party. What food would there be? Where would they have the party? Would there be a theme? How many people would they invite?

NOT FEELING HURT

Ask the children to write a letter to Daniel about how he should feel when he is not invited to a party. Use lots of positive words. At the end, ask a few children to share their letters and read them out to the group.

DISTRACTIONS

Get the children into twos and ask them to discuss things they could do, instead of going to a party they weren't invited to. Have a group discussion sharing those things.

Part 7

BULLYING

STICKS AND STONES

(ABOUT CRUEL WORDS AND HOW TO RISE ABOVE THEM)

GINNY'S STORY

EDUCATORS' NOTES

Suggested age for story – 8–11 years old

Children need to learn resilience when it comes to friendships and bullies. They need to be able to stand up for themselves and not let others make them feel bad about themselves. They need to know how to stand up to people who call them names.

If a child learns this type of resilience they will be able to cope with many different types of people and personalities and they will not be afraid of saying what they believe in and speaking up for what they know is wrong. This will be useful for them later on in life at secondary school or during their years in higher education and in the workplace.

All pre- and post-lesson exercises can be used for evaluation purposes if required.

LEARNING OUTCOMES

- Knowing what to say when others call you names.

- Don't take on board other people's 'negative' thoughts about the way you look.

- Be confident about who you are and what you look like.

- Protect your heart from cruel words.

- Understand that there will always be bullies but you don't have to be a victim.

INTRODUCTION STATEMENT

Today we are going to talk about friendship and bullies and how important it is to be confident when other people call you names and try to make you feel awful about the way you look. School life should be a good experience for everyone – a chance to learn new skills, make lots of friends and try new things. It should be a time in your life when you shouldn't have to worry about anything. It isn't a good experience for everyone though because some children are teased for the way they look or act and for the way they are. Maybe they are not the brightest child in the class or they stand out a bit more than the other children. Sometimes there is no reason at all; it's just the bully being mean.

Being teased or being bullied happens and it can make children feel terrible about themselves and sometimes not want to go to school. No child deserves to be teased or bullied.

People who like to tease others do it because they are unhappy with the way their own life is. They may be unhappy at home and so like to make other children unhappy at school. They try and make others feel rotten so they feel better about themselves. For some children, to be able to make another person upset whilst looking cool in front of their friends makes them feel powerful. Other children are jealous. There are so many reasons why some children are mean to others and most of the time we never really know the real reason.

We must not let the bullies win by letting them make us feel awful about who we are and how we feel about ourselves. We need to believe we are good people and stop the teasing quickly before it gets to be a bigger and more serious problem.

PRE- AND POST-LESSON EXERCISE

Ask the children if they feel confident about standing up to people calling them names. How many strategies do they know if someone calls them names? Before reading the story get them to write them down. At the end of the story get them to look over the list they have made and add any new ideas they have.

The girls that teased Ginny in the story I am going to read stopped what they were doing very quickly because she knew what to say and do.

GINNY'S STORY

OMG where do I start?

Worst few days. EVER!

Mum said I'm such a drama queen when I say that but see what you think.

It all started with Rachel.

New girl. Brainy. Great looking. Uber-popular. Funny… Sly. Cruel.

Sums it up. Doesn't it? Really?

Everyone was all over her from the moment she arrived.

Except me. And a few others I guess. But we never talked about it. Just saw her coming. Gave each other the look and moved away to get on with our already okay lives at school. Well, they had been okay.

Until Rachel arrived.

At the time it seemed like the whole of my class wanted to be best mates with Rachel.

Me and a few others crept around the outside of the ever-growing fan club. Kept our heads down and went on with our lives.

I never did fit into the 'popular' group. But actually once you've got used to the fact you're not in the cool group, the pressure to be a part of it disappears and, you know something? It's a much nicer place to be.

Once the pushing around for a place next to Rachel had stopped and Rachel settled in with her gang of four other girls, most of us breathed a sigh of relief.

I'd seen those programmes on the TV about the survival of the fittest in jungles and it didn't surprise me to see that the same bullies who had tormented the class for the past four years were now arm in arm with Rachel and strutting their stuff around the playground every break time while they boasted to everyone about their new-found friend.

A few months passed. I had almost forgotten about Rachel. Stupid really.

I should have known better.

There had always been this one girl in my class, Ashley, who had been the ringleader of whatever nastiness happened to anyone. Of course, she was one of Rachel's newly found BFFs and one lunch break I heard

Copyright © Naomi Richards and Julia Hague 2016

her voice drifting across the playground towards me as I sat talking to one of my friends, Jazz. Jazz dug me hard in the waist with her fingers and I looked up.

The gang of five, as we now called Rachel and her cronies, were heading in my direction.

Perfect.

Rachel's face had that 'look who's here' expression and Ashley had her arm linked into hers.

As always, Ashley's face was twisted into some sort of evil witch look and she spat her words out.

'Where'd you get that haircut, string bean? You look like a boy. An ugly, ugly boy. You need to take yourself to St Dominic's down the road. You'd fit in better with the boys.'

The five girls laughed loudly.

'This is a girls' school, in case your mother got a bit confused. You need to look like a girl to be here. You and your little friend certainly don't,' Rachel added.

I felt tears pricking my eyes. Hot and painful. I tried not to let one escape but it betrayed me and started heading down my cheek. An angry, hurt tear.

I was aware of the fact I was tall, skinny and had no shape.

Yet, most of the time I forgot. My friends, like Jazz, didn't care about what shape I was or anything. We just had fun. Great fun. The teasing and bullying up to now had been about my shape. Skinny beanpole. That was okay. I'd got over that. Accepted it.

My hair though hadn't ever entered into any of the taunts.

But I'd had a haircut at the weekend and this was the first day back. So I got noticed.

The hairdresser had suggested a nice short cut to match my shape and size. She layered it and said it would be fashionable and easy to do. I had been so happy. So happy.

I think that was it. I'd been so happy that the feeling of hurt at having that happiness taken away was more painful. I guess.

The gang laughed when they saw me cry. Then they walked away. I felt hate for them. Jazz sat silently beside me.

'That was sooo bad,' she whispered and then put her arm around me.

Copyright © Naomi Richards and Julia Hague 2016

I nodded.

Through the afternoon when we moved from class to class for our lessons, one of the gang would make sure they pushed their way past me and Jazz and whisper loudly.

'Boys shouldn't be here. You'll both get thrown out soon.'

My mum picked me up from school and straight away noticed I was quiet.

'Good day at school, Ginny?' she said as she kissed me on the cheek.

'Okay I guess.'

'Anyone notice your hair cut?'

'Oh yeah.'

'Great. Bet they liked it.'

'Not really. Wish you hadn't suggested it really,' I said quietly and then bit my tongue.

Wasn't Mum's fault. Although I wanted to blame her. Anyone. Then it would make it okay to be teased about it. 'Cos I hadn't had a hand in it. Been told to have it. But I knew I'd wanted it as much as Mum had wanted me to have it. But I was kind of clutching at straws.

'Why on earth not?' she said as we got into the car.

'Don't want to talk about it,' I replied.

'Okay well maybe later then,' Mum said. She knew I only talked about stuff when I was ready.

I did my homework and then watched a bit of TV.

At dinner Mum and Dad were talking about our summer holiday and where we were going.

'It's very hot where we're going so you're going to be glad your hair is short, Ginny,' Mum said cheerfully.

I moved the peas around my plate and didn't say anything. I had gone over and over in my mind what happened that day and stared at myself in the mirror.

I hated what I saw. I never had before. Now, because of Rachel and her cronies, I hated something that I had loved only a day earlier.

I decided that talking to Mum was a good option after all. She always had a great view on stuff.

When I'd finished, she settled back in her chair and folded her hands in her lap.

Copyright © Naomi Richards and Julia Hague 2016

'You know, Ginny. Girls like Rachel are bullies because they are trying to feel good about themselves. Saying mean things to others is a way of taking away from the bad feelings they have about something in their lives. We will never know what. But there will be something.

I know it's hard to ignore it when people say things to you like that but if you could try and understand that it's about them more than it is about you, you can step away from it.'

'I wanted to say mean things back to her but I think it would make them worse towards me,' I said.

'Two wrongs will never make a right, darling. You're just showing them that you care by acting the same as them. They are just words. Nothing else. Words. And they are coming from the mouths of people you don't even like. So you need to say to yourself that if you don't care for them, why do you care for what they say? Look I have a suggestion of what you can say to them. It worked for me when I was at school when I had this horrid girl named Sophie who started bullying me.'

I tossed and turned that night. Mum's suggestion was brilliant but I'll admit I was nervous about school and how Rachel and Ashley had made me feel. The following morning I went into school and went straight to Jazz. I told her what Mum's idea was and she grinned.

At break time, the gang made their way across the playground once more.

'If it isn't the wannabe boys,' Rachel taunted as she reached us. 'I thought I told you, you shouldn't be in this school.'

'We really don't care what you think anymore,' I said and stood up and raised my face to look Rachel straight in the eye.

Jazz stood up too next to me and she straightened her shoulders and put her hands on her waist and glared at them.

'See, we are both who we are and we're happy about it. We only care about what our friends think. Not what people like you think. You don't matter to us. So if you've got something to say to us, we won't hear it from now on. Ever. It will be like your voice hits an invisible bubble around us and it won't reach our ears. So don't bother saying stuff anymore.' I looked at Jazz after I said it and then I stared hard at Rachel again and didn't blink.

Rachel stood for a minute and then turned on her heels.

Copyright © Naomi Richards and Julia Hague 2016

'You still look like boys,' she said over her shoulder.

'Did you hear something, Ginny?' Jazz said to me as we both sat down.

'Might have been an insect buzzing,' I said and smiled.

The teasing didn't stop for ages. Of course. It lessened but Rachel and her friends were too stupid to take the hint that it wasn't affecting Jazz and me anymore. They had to keep trying. After all, it's the survival of the fittest in their eyes and backing down wasn't an option. But thanks to my mum's suggestion, Jazz and I got to the point where we actually didn't really hear what they said because we weren't interested anymore so the words didn't hurt us.

Words really are just that. They come from people's mouths and sometimes they are wise and sometimes they are just total rubbish. It is best only to listen to the people who you care about and ignore those who you don't. If we don't care for the bullies then we should not care for their words either.

So yeah, maybe I'm a drama queen.

Copyright © Naomi Richards and Julia Hague 2016

NOTES TO SUPPORT THE DISCUSSION

There are many other ways Ginny could have dealt with the mean girls. One thing she could have done is ignore them totally so they got bored of calling her names. She could also have agreed with what the girls were saying. For example, when she was told 'You look like a boy,' she could have answered, 'Yes. I do and I quite like it.'

I think we should always remember that whatever someone says to us, we don't let it turn our good mood into a bad mood. We need to be able to switch on the button that says, 'I am not going to let these words hurt me. Those girls are clearly jealous of me being so fantastic. I am not going to let them make me feel bad.'

Understanding that children who are bullies are not usually happy in their own lives can help us to walk away from the situation and ignore them. We should never allow someone else to take away our own happiness just because they are unhappy.

DISCUSSION QUESTIONS TO ASK THE CHILDREN

- What do you think about the story?
- What do you think about what Ginny did?
- What did you learn from it?
- Do you think you would have done something different to Ginny? If so, what?
- How do you think Rachel would have felt having someone stand up to her?
- If Rachel had tried to become your friend and you knew that she was a bully what would you have done?

ACTIVITIES TO DO WITH THE CHILDREN

HELPING SOMEONE LIKE GINNY

Ask the children to write a letter to Ginny with the advice they would give her. Include in it how she could feel better about the way she looked.

TAKE A LOOK AT YOURSELF

Get the children to draw pictures of themselves and write next to them the things they love about their body or their face. They should be told to write down at least five things.

STICKS AND STONES

The story is called sticks and stones. Ask the group to make up a poem that is about names that will never hurt you.

LESSON LEARNT

Put the children into groups and ask them to make up a lesson plan to teach other children about bullies and teasing.

CHINESE WHISPERS

(ABOUT REALIZING WHISPERS COULD BE ABOUT ANYTHING)

ISABELLE'S STORY

EDUCATORS' NOTES

Suggested age for story – 8–10 years old

Children need to understand that they are not always the subject of gossip from other people and that 'guessing' what others are talking about can damage the way they feel about themselves. If a child has healthy self-esteem they will realize that when their friends and peers are whispering they could be talking about anything. It most definitely does not have to be about them.

Children are allowed to talk in groups. That is something all friendship groups do and children who see others whispering should not be upset by it.

This story should encourage children to think more positively about what is going on around them, and to feel more confident in their friendships. If they do this, then the confidence will spill into other areas of their lives and will increase their happiness.

All pre- and post-lesson exercises can be used for evaluation purposes if required.

LEARNING OUTCOMES

- Mindreading is dangerous.
- Friends are allowed to talk together and look around.
- Not everything is as it seems.
- Whispers can turn into good surprises.

INTRODUCTION STATEMENT

It can be tempting sometimes to huddle into a group and talk about something. It could be discussing a TV programme you watched last night. It could be to talk about a teacher who is in close range and you don't want them to hear. It can be very tempting to whisper. But whispers can be quite dangerous to friends looking in who are not a part of the 'secret'. That's what whispers look like don't they? They look like a secret is being shared. But they are not always. They can be something else – maybe something quite innocent that a person does not want to share with everyone – maybe something embarrassing happened to them or maybe a surprise is being planned.

When we whisper we need to be aware that we may hurt someone's feelings and make them feel left out or self-conscious.

PRE- AND POST-LESSON EXERCISE

Before reading the story ask the children to write down a sentence about how they feel when they see two friends whispering together. After the story, ask them how they would feel in the future.

Okay, let's find out what happened to Isabelle in the story of 'Chinese Whispers'. It's all about whispering and how people can get upset by it and behave strangely.

ISABELLE'S STORY

There's this game you sometimes play at parties.

The first person whispers something to the person sitting next to them.

Then that person whispers what they heard to the person next to them.

And this continues around the circle until it gets back to the final person, who shares what they heard with the people playing.

At the end, everyone laughs because what the final person says is never EVER what the first person said.

Funny, huh?

Yeah, well in a party I guess it is.

Everyone's having fun and no one kind of cares what was said in the first place.

Because it's not about anyone.

It's just fun.

But when it's not in a party.

When the whispers are about you.

Or you imagine they are.

Then it's not fun.

Sometimes we can get it wrong too. You thought the whispers were about you but they weren't.

But because you thought they were, you treated people differently.

Got angry and resentful that people were obviously talking about you.

That every glance in your direction.

Or heads bowed together.

Or giggling and looking in your direction.

Was about you.

And not in a nice way.

And then suddenly you find out you were wrong.

That it was all in your mind.

How come I know so much about all of this?

I know you're thinking how self-centred I must have been.

Copyright © Naomi Richards and Julia Hague 2016

Thinking everything was about me.

But I wasn't.

I was just nervous.

And shy.

And scared of what people thought about me.

So when they looked at me and talked.

I assumed it was bad stuff.

Otherwise why would they be whispering and then stopping when I came near?

Then one day I got a wake-up call and found out that not all whispering is bad.

That whispering can be good.

I'd been about two years at the school I'm at now.

I had a couple of friends despite being shy.

My best friends were Grace and Abbie.

I would find them in the playground whispering together and then abruptly stopping when I got close.

I didn't think too much about it at first. They were my closest friends. I trusted them.

One day I saw them and they were in a group with other girls who I also liked but was not as friendly with as Grace and Abbie. They were all whispering and giggling but stopped when they saw me.

I must have blushed or something because Abbie ran over and took my arm and steered me away from the group, chatting about the homework we had to do that night.

Before I knew it I had been propelled into another corridor and away from the group.

This happened a few times and I got more and more nervous.

I started to avoid Abbie and Grace.

I knew that something was going on. Something that made me uneasy.

I had even convinced myself that everyone was talking about me.

And it was not a good feeling considering my birthday was at the weekend. It was a special one, my tenth, and my mum had suggested I invite Abbie and Grace to go ice skating and then for pizza.

Copyright © Naomi Richards and Julia Hague 2016

But when I asked them, they said they were busy. Perhaps another day.

I was so hurt. I wanted to go out on my actual birthday, not another day.

They looked so guilty when they said no. Like they were doing something else and knew they should have been with me for my birthday treat.

Mum said she and Dad would take me and my brother. 'Don't worry,' she said. 'You can go with Abbie and Grace another time.'

So Sunday came and we went to the rink.

When we arrived I saw a couple of girls from school skating. They tried not to make eye contact. So I looked away too.

Then I saw some more. How come there were so many girls from my class there that day? It did not make sense.

All of a sudden there was this loud cheer and clapping.

I turned around to see what was happening.

Mum was smiling and Dad had my brother on his shoulders. He was grinning from ear to ear.

Standing in the doorway were Abbie and Grace and the girls I had seen earlier from school.

Some of the same girls who had been whispering with Abbie and Grace recently.

They ran over and hugged me and shouted 'Happy Birthday' and the others all crowded around and handed me presents.

There were balloons and cake and so many of the girls from my class.

I couldn't believe my eyes.

Mum said that Abbie and Grace had asked her if they could arrange a surprise party for me.

So they had to say no when I'd invited them so they could surprise me.

At the end of the party Abbie sidled up to me.

'You were so difficult to keep a secret from, Izzie. Every time we were whispering it was about the arrangements.'

I've never looked at people whispering in the same way again.

When someone is whispering and maybe giggling about something, even if they are looking at me, it doesn't mean it's bad. And it probably isn't about me.

But if it is…well look how my birthday turned out because of whispering.

Copyright © Naomi Richards and Julia Hague 2016

NOTES TO SUPPORT THE DISCUSSION

Isabelle was really upset that her friends seemed to be talking about and not including her. Good friends always include others so it made her feel unhappy that she was not part of her friends' chats. It takes a child with a very healthy self-esteem to know that even if they are being whispered about, they are not being talked about in a negative way.

There may have been another way for the surprise to be organized so that Isabelle did not see the whispering. Perhaps the mums could have discussed it on the phone or via email. Isabelle would never have had reason to doubt her friends then.

Whispering can be seen as rude, as it makes others feel left out. It does not matter what the whispering is about – it still upsets other people. Children need to be considerate of other people's feelings. It can also make children question who they are and, like Isabelle, they can pull away from a group because they believe the whispers are about them and are not nice.

DISCUSSION QUESTIONS TO ASK THE CHILDREN

- What do you think of Isabelle's story?
- What did you learn from the story?
- Do you think Isabelle had a right to be upset?
- Would you have felt the same?
- What would you have done if you were Isabelle and saw your friends whispering?
- Could they have arranged the birthday surprise another way?

ACTIVITIES TO DO WITH THE CHILDREN

GETTING POETIC

Ask the children to make up a poem about the dangers of whispering using the letters of the word 'WHISPERS'.

IN SECRET

Get the children into groups of four and ask them to plan a party for one of their best friends. Get them to include all the little details of where, when, the theme and, most importantly, how they would arrange it without them knowing.

FEELING STRONG

Ask the children to write down the positive thoughts they could have in the future when they see one of their friends whispering. Can they write down at least three thoughts?

STANDING UP TO THE WHISPERERS

In twos, get the children to role play what they would say if they saw one of their best friends whispering about them. Remembering what happened in the story, what language would they use and what kind of attitude would they have? Both children should have a go.

STORY TWENTY-FIVE

CONNECTING

(ABOUT BEING BULLIED ON SOCIAL MEDIA)

ADAM'S STORY

EDUCATORS' NOTES

Suggested age for story – 8–10 years old

Having a laptop or tablet is becoming more important to a child of this age. Their friends are using them to do their schoolwork, to play games and also to connect with other people. Social media is no longer something children in secondary school use. Children in Year 4 and upwards are using Instagram, MSN, Skype, etc. They are using it to speak to extended family and so they want to use them with their friends.

There is a dangerous side to social media as well as the prevalent bullying issue. Children need to understand these dangers so they can protect themselves. They need to learn whom to trust online and through experience they will become more internet savvy and streetwise, increasing their general awareness of what is going on around them. Children need to be streetwise and knowledgeable about social media before they move to secondary school so that they are confident and not scared of using it. They will be able to bring this confidence into online and offline communication with friends.

All pre- and post-lesson exercises can be used for evaluation purposes if required.

LEARNING OUTCOMES

- Make sure you know who you are talking to on social media.
- Challenge people you are not sure about.

- Make sure an adult knows what you are doing on social media.

- If someone is not nice stop speaking to them online.

- Only add people to groups if you have met them in person and you like them.

INTRODUCTION STATEMENT

It is great to be able to go online and have a chat about your day, laugh about what you got up to in lessons and find out who has been doing what at school. Social media is brilliant for that, so when you get bullied on the internet it takes away the fun.

Sometimes, especially when playing online games, we don't always know who we are talking to. We may think we know, but anyone can make up a silly name and say nasty things to other people whilst hiding behind a screen. No one will know it is them – well, that is what they think. Bullies do get found out. If you are being bullied or someone is unkind on social media you have to tell an adult it is happening. Bullying online is wrong and cowardly and must be reported.

PRE- AND POST-LESSON EXERCISE
What do the children not like about speaking to their friends on the computer? Get them to make a list before the story. Ask them after the story to add to the list in a different coloured pen. The list should be longer after the story.

As you may have guessed the story is about bullying online. Let's find out what happened to Adam, who really wanted to be using instant messaging like his friends.

ADAM'S STORY

I thought my world was complete when Mum and Dad bought me my own laptop last year.

I was so excited. No longer did I have to use Mum's or Dad's when they were not using theirs. Which seemed to be never.

There were conditions on using it though.

I had to use it in the kitchen. A place where they could see exactly what I was doing.

I really wanted to use it for Instagram, Skype, email, MSN.

All the things my friends were using.

I pleaded with Dad to let me.

At first he didn't.

He said the computer wasn't for that. It was for me to use for research for my school projects.

Then one day there was this test at school and all my friends had somehow found out about it the night before.

It was because they'd been talking about it online and of course I didn't know.

I came home from school really upset because I hadn't prepared and all my friends had.

Dad tried reasoning with me that surprise tests were meant to be surprise. That they tested what you knew and not what you'd prepared the night before.

I wasn't happy.

I felt left out. If only I had MSN. I pleaded with Dad again to have it.

Dad caved under my whingeing and Mum helped me set up a private account on MSN. We left out all the personal details and she made the account private so that only people I invited to be friends could see what I said.

At least that's what I thought.

It felt safe and for the first few weeks it was fun.

After a month I asked if it was now okay for me to use my laptop upstairs in my room.

Copyright © Naomi Richards and Julia Hague 2016

I remember Mum taking my shoulders and looking me in the eye and making me promise that chatting to my friends on my laptop would only be after homework and never after I went to bed.

I promised.

But you get sucked in.

I'd be looking up something for my history project and one of my friends would pop up in a window at the bottom of the screen and start talking.

It was too tempting not to answer them.

Then about a month ago it started.

I was finishing a poem for English the next day. I was about to hit the print button so that it would print downstairs on Dad's printer.

A chat bubble appeared at the bottom of the screen.

I stared at what it was saying.

You're the most unpopular boy in the class.

I looked at the name on the bubble.

I didn't know it.

I forgot about printing and clicked the chat.

Who are you?

As I typed, I wasn't sure I wanted to know.

They all hate you.

I felt myself go red as I typed my reply.

I don't know you.

I was hurting a lot by now. Maybe it was a mistake. Someone thought I was someone I wasn't.

Yes you do.

I felt cold. I knew the person who was saying these horrid things?

I closed the laptop down.

I had messages like that daily.

I didn't want Dad to take away the laptop but I wanted to talk to him or Mum about it.

But I thought that if I told either of them they would take it away.

I didn't sleep well.

After two weeks I couldn't bear it any longer and I told Dad.

Copyright © Naomi Richards and Julia Hague 2016

He told me to tell him the next time it happened.

He didn't take away the laptop.

Phew.

But he and Mum did insist on the laptop only being used downstairs again.

Actually I didn't mind. The nasty chat had really freaked me out.

So the next time the chat bubble appeared and the nasty things were being said I called Dad over.

He came up and opened the chat and then printed it out.

I didn't really know what he was doing but my dad knows his way around computers and after about half an hour he wrote something down and closed down the laptop.

'Adam, has anyone else had messages like this?' He asked.

I didn't know.

But then I hadn't exactly spoken to anyone else about it. Not even my best friend.

Dad explained that it was important that the person was stopped.

He said that it was possible they might be saying worse things to other friends who might not have confided in their parents.

He was right. I had not thought of that.

The next day, Dad, Mum and I had a meeting with my class teacher and head teacher.

The head said that if anything like this ever happened again I should always tell my class teacher.

He also said that, thanks to Dad printing it all out, they knew who it was and that he was going to have a talk with the boy and his parents.

The boy called Jonah, who was in the class above me and my friends, was suspended that day.

That same day our ICT teacher gave us a talk on social media and bullying and how to protect ourselves.

Mum and Dad didn't take away the laptop.

But I wasn't allowed to use it anywhere other than the kitchen or the lounge.

But that was okay and I learnt something.

Copyright © Naomi Richards and Julia Hague 2016

Social media can be great as long as you are talking to friends.

But sometimes you don't know who else is in on a chat.

Not really.

When you can't see them they could be anyone as they are hiding behind an identity on there.

And bullies think that's great.

That they can hide behind a name.

And bully.

And they think they won't get into trouble because no one will find out who they are.

But if you talk to your parents or your teachers when you have a problem online they can help you sort it out.

And in the end bullies really can't hide.

Because there's always someone who will find out who they are.

Just like my dad did.

Copyright © Naomi Richards and Julia Hague 2016

NOTES TO SUPPORT THE DISCUSSION

Adam learnt a hard lesson and possibly he was a bit too trusting. He thought that everyone he was linked to on social media was his friend and did not think too much about people being able to speak to him who he did not know. He did the right thing by telling his parents when he received the horrible messages. Children must tell a parent or an adult they can trust.

Bullies like to hide behind a screen as it makes them feel good about making someone else feel awful about themselves. Some children may think they will never be found out but it is very easy to find out who sends messages. A policeman or someone who really knows computers can find it out easily.

It may have been a good idea for his mum or dad to be linked into his account so that they could keep an eye on what he was doing and see the messages going back and forth. That would have been a good safety net for him since he was new to chatting online with his friends.

DISCUSSION QUESTIONS TO ASK THE CHILDREN

- How do you feel about the story?

- Did Adam do the right thing by telling his dad? Why?

- Would you have done the same thing?

- What would you tell your friend to do if they were being bullied on social media?

- Were Adam's parents right to allow him to go on social media?

- Are you on social media and if so how do your parents restrict the time you spend on it?

ACTIVITIES TO DO WITH THE CHILDREN

GOOD AND BAD

Put up two sheets of flipchart paper – one for good and one for bad – and get the children to shout out the good and bad parts of social media. Which list is longer? Ask the children to justify why they put each point on the list.

HELPING THE BULLY

Get the children to imagine they found out their best friend was the online bully and to write them an anonymous letter about what they have done to get them to think about their actions.

PROTECTION

What can you do to protect yourself online? Ask the children to design a poster to remind people of the dangers of bullying online.

RULE MAKERS

Ask the children to pretend that they are the parent of a child who has just been given access to a computer. Get them to write down five rules they would have to make sure their child was safe on the internet. Afterwards get them to call them out. The completed list of suggestions could be made into a handout for the children to take home.

SAFETY NET

(ABOUT KNOWING WHO TO TALK TO IN TIMES OF NEED)

JAKE'S STORY

EDUCATORS' NOTES

Suggested age for story – 9–11 years old

Often a child will be too scared to share their problems or their worries with their parents or another grown-up for fear of getting into trouble. They do not often know how the grown-up is going to respond or if they will even be able to help and so try to deal with situations themselves. Dealing with a problem alone is not always easy to do, especially when the problem gets bigger and the child realizes they need someone to help them before they get into really big trouble.

Children need to know that parents are there to help and advise them and that they will support them in times of need. Children will feel less stressed if they do share their worries and problems with their parents.

Being stressed can have an impact on all areas of their life. It can impact the child's mood at school and at home. Lifting that stress and sharing their problems can allow them to be a child and not feel that they have to cope alone.

All pre- and post-lesson exercises can be used for evaluation purposes if required.

LEARNING OUTCOMES

- Worries are better shared.

- Parents and other grown-ups can have lots of ideas of how to help with issues.

- It is always best to tell the truth.

- Mums and dads often have good advice.

- Tell someone your worries before they get bigger.

INTRODUCTION STATEMENT

Sometimes we get told information that we do not know what to do with. Someone can tell us something that can make us feel guilty and a part of something we don't want to be part of. For example, someone may tell us a secret about something they did wrong and then ask us to keep it. We know we shouldn't but we do because they are our friend. The secret then gets bigger and we know that in the end we may get into trouble. So who do we turn to when we do not know what to do? The best people are our parents or another grown-up that we trust. Both are there to help with our worries and problems and often have great ideas of how to solve them. When we share our worries we feel more relaxed and happier as we know someone can help us. It is better to share a problem than feel horrible feelings about yourself or feel nervous and anxious.

PRE- AND POST-LESSON EXERCISE

Before the story, ask the children who they turn to when they have a problem and how likely it is for them to go to their mum or dad. After the story, find out in percentage terms how much that has gone up.

Jake felt scared when he had to lie about where he was one particular time so that he did not get a friend's brother in trouble. He did not like lying but also did not know where to seek help. Let's hear his story and who he asked for help in the end.

JAKE'S STORY

When I was very little I would climb on my mum or dad's knee when something was wrong and tell them what I was sad about.

They'd give me a cuddle and make everything better.

But as I got older and I was at school, climbing on my parents' knees upset wasn't something I did.

For a start I thought it was a bit babyish. If my older brother caught me doing it he would have laughed at me.

Secondly, and, as I discovered later, wrongly, I wasn't sure if Mum and Dad would understand my worries or if they would even be able to help.

And so when something went wrong last week I kept my problem to myself.

How stupid.

Afterwards I tried to work out why I hadn't asked for help.

I think it was because I really didn't know how to start talking to my parents about it.

And I was scared.

So I didn't.

My problems had all started one morning that week at school.

My best friend, Freddie had steered me into a corner of the playground and told me he had a big problem.

Freddie's older brother, Julian, was in big trouble.

He'd been out with a gang of friends the day before and they'd broken some windows and sprayed graffiti.

Julian had come back home and sworn Freddie to say he was with him and not with the gang if anyone asked.

Freddie was so scared of saying 'No' that he'd said 'Okay' – he'd back Julian up.

But what Freddie then told me, made my heart sink.

Julian had also made Freddie agree to include me in on the whole thing.

So if I was asked I was supposed to say that Julian had been with me and Freddie that afternoon after school, when I knew that he hadn't been.

Copyright © Naomi Richards and Julia Hague 2016

We'd been in the park playing football alone.

Julian knew that.

He also knew that Freddie would be too scared to say no to him. I guess he thought the same about me.

To my shame I realized he was right. I was scared of Julian.

But I was also scared silly about the thought of lying and being found out.

And I wasn't comfortable with letting Julian get away with what he'd done.

I think Freddie knew that I wasn't happy. He admitted he wasn't either but he said it was for the best to just agree. 'No one would know we weren't playing football with Julian.' 'Nothing could happen.'

My thoughts just kept on circling around and around.

I couldn't concentrate that evening.

I was desperate to tell Mum or Dad or both.

Get help.

Have someone give me advice.

I didn't know what to do.

But I said nothing.

As the week wore on and nothing happened I began to think nothing was going to come of it.

No one asked me anything.

Life went on as normal.

I started to relax.

But then it happened.

Freddie came into school and told me the police had contacted his parents and Julian had told them he hadn't been with the gang who'd done the damage. That he'd been with Freddie and me instead.

Freddie had backed up Julian's story but the police wanted to speak to me.

Freddie said his parents had given the police my parents' details and they were going to contact them to chat to me.

As I climbed into the car after school, I didn't wait for my mum to drive off, I blurted out the whole story. I said it so fast that my mum looked around at me puzzled. I wasn't making a lot of sense. My brother just sat and stared at me.

Copyright © Naomi Richards and Julia Hague 2016

Mum told me to hold what I was trying to say until we got home.

That evening was the longest evening I've ever experienced.

Mum listened carefully to what I said.

Her face changed from annoyed to worried to sympathetic.

She asked me why I hadn't told them earlier – asked for help before now. What was I thinking?

I didn't know how to answer any of it.

Mum phoned Dad and he came home from work early.

Dad said that I had to tell the truth. That 'whatever happened to Julian was his own fault'. That 'involving two younger boys in his lies made matters worse'.

I was worried for Freddie.

He'd lied.

But Dad said that if I told the truth then it was better for Freddie. If we'd both lied and Julian had got away with it things would be worse.

So, when the police knocked on the door and they asked me, I told them the truth. I told them everything.

I felt this huge weight lift off me. Like a black cloud had been sitting on my head and it had now blown away.

After they'd gone, Dad and Mum sat down with me.

What Dad told me I will never forget.

Ever.

He said that parents are the safety nets for their kids. They will catch you if you fall and stop you hitting the ground hard.

And no matter what happens in your life you can always turn to them for help.

'And tell them anything.'

Dad said that if Freddie had been too frightened to talk to his parents about Julian then it was very sad, but he could always have turned to his teacher at school.

Dad said that some problems are bigger than we are and that when we share them we halve them.

I like that thought.

Copyright © Naomi Richards and Julia Hague 2016

NOTES TO SUPPORT THE DISCUSSION

Jake did not like having to lie for his friend's brother. He knew it was wrong and did not want to be a part of it. He felt quite strongly that Julian should not get away with it yet he did not want to get him into trouble either. Jake felt unhappy and stressed, which is not a good way to be, so he made a brave decision to speak to his mum when he realized how serious it was getting. We may think it is better to keep secrets safe but when they have an impact on more than one person it is best to tell a grown up and they will support you. We have to think of what is right and do the right thing.

When stuck with dilemmas we need to be able to think them through and look for the best solution. Often this means talking to a grown-up and trusting them with what we know. It is better to share the problem than keep it inside, especially when the problem could involve the police or have serious consequences.

DISCUSSION QUESTIONS TO ASK THE CHILDREN

- What is your impression of Jake?

- How do you think he handled the situation?

- What would you have done differently?

- How do you think Jake felt knowing that secret? And how do you think he felt when he told his mum?

- Have you ever had a problem that you have kept to yourself? How did you feel?

- How do you feel about telling mum and dad about your problems? Why?

- If you couldn't talk to your parents for some reason, which other adult would you trust to speak to?

- Would you lie for a friend?

ACTIVITIES TO DO WITH THE CHILDREN

SHARING PROBLEMS

Ask the children to write down on post-its the problems they would speak to their mum or dad about and the problems they wouldn't. Put them on a wall in two lists and then use them as a discussion point.

DRAMA

Get a group of children to act out Jake's story but get them to change the endings to:

- Jake telling his mum and dad straight away
- Jake speaking to Julian and saying he is not going to lie
- Jake telling Freddie that he wouldn't lie for his brother when he first told him
- Jake doing something else. What can the children come up with?

SECRETS

Get the children to write a poem about secrets and the impact they can have on your life.

HEADSPACE

Get the children to draw a picture of a head and then write within it the feelings that they would have if they knew someone had done something wrong and wasn't getting justice.

Part 8

FITTING IN

THE NUMBERS GAME

(ABOUT COMPARING YOURSELF TO OTHERS ACADEMICALLY)

CHARLIE'S STORY

EDUCATORS' NOTES

Suggested age for story – 10–11 years old

Many girls and boys feel under pressure to work really hard to get the best marks in their class or in their year at school. This pressure can come from a mum or dad telling their children that they need to be at the top of the class in every subject and by making comparisons between their child and their friends. It can also come from their peer group who are also under pressure themselves.

Some children feel as if they cannot work any harder than they are already doing and it can make them unwell and panicky. Children in this situation need to vocalize that they feel 'stressed' so that their teachers and parents can help them.

If children focus less on being the best and being competitive academically, they will be happier with what they are doing and achieving. They will enjoy life more and focus on what is really important – having fun with friends and family.

All pre- and post-lesson exercises can be used for evaluation purposes if required.

LEARNING OUTCOMES

- Children need to vocalize if they feel pressure.

- They need to understand that some children are competitive.

- They need to know that trying their best is enough.

- They shouldn't compare themselves to others academically.

- They cannot be good at everything.

INTRODUCTION STATEMENT

We are going to discuss pressure today. The kind of pressure other people can put on us, as they want us to get the best mark in the class or year group. This pressure can come from Mum or Dad because they want you to do well or it may come from you or from your friends who are fiercely competitive.

We need to be realistic with how well we can do in a subject and understand that we may never get top marks in it. There is a line between trying hard and doing well, and trying too hard. If you think about the subjects at school, which ones do you think you push yourself too hard in? Which ones make you unhappy because you are not doing as well as you want to?

The story I am going to read is about Charlie. Charlie felt lots of pressure from his mum and dad. They wanted him to be the best at everything and had a particular school they wanted him to go to after Year 6. Charlie did not want to let them down but he knew he was not going to get into their chosen school. He tried hard but he was also realistic about who he was and what he wanted.

PRE- AND POST-LESSON EXERCISE

Before reading the story ask the children to each write down one academic subject that they feel pressure to achieve in or one activity where they feel the pressure to be the best. After the story ask them to go back to the sheet and write down ways in which they could change the way they feel about that subject/activity.

Let's listen to Charlie's story.

CHARLIE'S STORY

Mum and Dad keep telling me that 'working hard starts when you go to school and only ends when you retire'. The first time they said it I remember thinking that I couldn't think of being as old as my granddad, who had just retired.

They also said that 'the most important thing was to be the best at everything,' and getting the best grades in class. Passing my piano grades faster than Nathan whose mum talks to my mum.

Oh and, of course, sport. You can't be a boy and not like sport.

Apparently.

So if you like it you have to be good at it. Dad says so. I think he wants to see me on TV playing football at Wembley or something.

But that's hard. I can't be the best at everything.

I mean, if I was, I'd grow up to be some football hero who was a concert pianist while at the exact same time solving some really hard equations, which meant we could all get to the moon in an hour.

Seriously. Is anyone good at everything? Anyone?

Last term I got 80 per cent in my science test and I was sixth in the class. Pretty good I thought. Nope, my parents were not interested.

'It's not the grade but where you are placed in the class that matters.' Dad wasn't in the mood for arguing.

'What about my piano exam last month? Mrs Foster said it was the highest mark she'd seen at that level for a long time.'

'Piano is all well and good but it's not going to get you into a good university to be a doctor, now, is it?' Dad continued. 'It's nice, but it's not maths or science.'

A little picture opened up in my head. I was a concert pianist on stage playing to tons of clapping and cheering. I bowed and took the applause. It felt good. Eat your heart out doctors of this world.

My lovely daydream was interrupted by my mum's voice chiming in.

'Talking about your piano. I meant to tell you that Nathan Crowley is a grade higher than you. His mum said he practises at least 40 minutes a

Copyright © Naomi Richards and Julia Hague 2016

night. I think you should practise more every night, dear. You don't want to be left behind.'

A few weeks later we all faced the horror, also known as the race, of the entrance exams to get into the best secondary school.

The usual suspects in my class made plenty of noise bragging about the schools they were sitting for. The exams their parents had entered them into.

My heart sank. The stress. The pressure.

The pressure came from my mum and dad. They had a school in mind and I just had to go there. Dad said the sports facilities were fantastic. Especially the football.

Had anyone asked me where I wanted to go? Nope.

Were they interested in where my friends were going? Nope.

Did I care about football? Nope.

The pressure got worse.

I started comparing myself to others in my class. Just like Mum and Dad told me I should. I'd never really done it before and I didn't like it but if I didn't get into the school Mum and Dad wanted I'd never hear the end of it.

Before this pressure I'd only ever felt good when I did well and I just felt resigned to the fact I couldn't be good at everything. I used to be comfortable being me. Now I wasn't sure anymore. My mum and dad were confusing me. Be good at everything. Be better than everyone.

I felt like I was in some sort of race and if I lost I'd hate myself.

And my parents would hate me too.

Then, one rainy morning it was like this light bulb went off in my head.

I wasn't like Nathan. I was me. Just me. Okay me. And that was alright.

I don't know what made me feel like that. The change back to me. I think it's because trying to be someone I wasn't couldn't go on forever. It's like wearing a mask or something that doesn't fit. The mask slipped off me that morning and the person who was trying to be perfect slipped off with it. Does that make sense?

I was me. Charlie. The boy who was great at history and English and even liked maths. Yeah, that's right. Maths. Science sometimes. Didn't love them. Wasn't top at them. But I liked them.

Copyright © Naomi Richards and Julia Hague 2016

Me – the boy who dreamt of playing his piano in front of thousands because he'd be sharing it with the world.

Me – the boy who didn't like football.

So I sat my exams and I did okay. I didn't get any scholarship and the sporty school my mum and dad had desperately wanted turned me down, but that was okay because I was secretly pleased.

I did get the prize for history at the end of the school year and was asked to play my piano in front of everyone. Everyone clapped and I felt good about it and Mum and Dad looked so proud of me.

For a moment anyway.

If they'd only accepted what I was good at instead of wanting me to be the best at everything they'd have realized that I'm pretty great as I am.

Doctor…? No thanks. I don't know what I'm going to be yet. But I have a feeling I'm going to end up being something I want to be rather than what someone else wants me to be.

And that is the coolest thing of all.

Copyright © Naomi Richards and Julia Hague 2016

NOTES TO SUPPORT THE DISCUSSION

It is important that children are able to share with their parents what they want and have their thoughts considered. If not, then they will follow their parents' path and be unhappy. They need to share what they like and if they feel under pressure tell their mum and dad how they feel so they can back off a bit.

This story is all about being academic and doesn't focus on practical skills. Both are important, but we do not need to put ourselves under pressure to do well at something when it is just not a strength of ours. We need to be realistic and do our best. Charlie realized he was fine the way he was and knew he had to find his own path, even if his mum and dad wanted something else for him.

The story also focuses on working hard but does not mention relaxing. Talk to the children about their other activities. Suggest that if they feel that they are doing too much and do not have enough time to relax maybe they could speak to Mum or Dad about dropping an activity – one that they don't enjoy that much.

DISCUSSION QUESTIONS TO ASK THE CHILDREN

- What lessons did you learn from the story?
- Do you think Charlie could have done something different?
- Have you ever felt like Charlie?
- What would you do if your parents put this kind of pressure on you? What would you say to them?
- Are you competitive? If so, why is it important to you how others do?
- What advice would you give Charlie?

ACTIVITIES TO DO WITH THE CLASS

BEING REALISTIC

Get the children to think about this term and what they want to improve on. Having something to aim for is fab but the aim has to be realistic. Ask them to write down what they want to be better at and how they can do it.

SUBJECTS OF STRENGTH

Put up flipchart paper around the room listing each subject that the children do and give everyone three post-it notes. Get the children to write down their top three subjects they do best at and then stick them up on the relevant flipchart paper. Discuss the differences on each sheet and see that not everyone is great at the same thing.

HOPES AND DREAMS

Ask the children to think about their dream job. What qualifications do they think they would need and what kind of person would they need to be? Ask the children to get creative and make a poster listing the qualities and experience they would need to have.

THE DOWNSIDE OF BEING COMPETITIVE

Ask the children to form small groups and together make a list of the downsides of being competitive and comparing themselves to others. Share the lists with the group.

LETTER HOME

Ask the children to write a letter to Charlie's parents explaining that he is feeling under pressure. In the letter they should suggest ways in which his parents could support the things he is good at.

AFTER YOU

(ABOUT PUTTING OTHERS BEFORE YOURSELF)

NIALL'S STORY

EDUCATORS' NOTES

Suggested age for story – 7–9 years old

One of the nicest traits children can have is kindness. Children need to learn to be kind and sometimes put others before themselves. They may not always realize why they are doing something kind but at the same time it feels like the right thing to do.

There does not have to be an ulterior motive for kindness. Kindness makes other people feel good, as they know the other person is putting them before themselves. It shows consideration and thoughtfulness. When children are kind they are looked at in a positive light and others see them as being nice people. People will be kind back and remember them for what they did. They will be asked to help out more at school and at home and possibly be given more responsibility. Being kind also boosts positive self-esteem.

All pre- and post-lesson exercises can be used for evaluation purposes if required.

LEARNING OUTCOMES

- It does not cost anything to be kind.

- We never know the outcome of kindness.

- It feels good to be kind.

- When someone is considerate it makes the recipient feel good.

INTRODUCTION STATEMENT

It is very easy to do what you want to do and to go along with what your friends want. It takes a different type of person to think of other people outside of your friendship group and their needs.

We may also be asked to do something that we don't want to do by a grown-up. For example, being asked to be in a group as part of a lesson and not being in that group with your friends. When asked, think about the reason why the grown-up has asked you and don't always think of yourself and how awful it will be for you. There is always a reason why the grown-up asked and there will be a benefit to someone.

PRE- AND POST-LESSON EXERCISE

Ask the children, 'When you are asked by the teacher to be in a pair with someone you don't like or to sit next to someone who is not in your friendship group, what is the first thought you have?' Ask them to write it down pre-story. After the story ask the children again to see if their thought process has changed.

So, today's story is all about being considerate and doing what you are asked to do without knowing the reason why. This happened to Niall and he went along with it.

NIALL'S STORY

At first I thought I should have been like Liam, my friend, who wouldn't give up his place in the queue.

He didn't want me to.

Got really cross with me.

Because we didn't end up sitting together.

But after the show was over I was glad I had given it up.

Really glad.

You see the school had booked for our class and the Year 4s to go to the Christmas pantomime.

We were all so excited.

Mainly because it was the day before we were breaking up for the Christmas holidays.

No one was concentrating in class. All everyone could think about was the pantomime.

After that we would go home and then the next day was half a day of fun really.

Then it was the Christmas holidays. Yippee!

So standing in the queue in the cold outside the theatre didn't bother anyone really.

The queue moved slowly into the theatre.

Liam and I were the next two to go through the curtain and get the last of the front row seats when Mrs Oliver, Class Four's teacher, spoke to Liam.

'Liam, can you sit in row two please? I'd like Lexi to sit in the front row.'

Liam pulled a face.

Lexi was older than us.

'Oh please, Mrs Oliver, I want to sit with Justin and Niall. Justin's just gone in so if I go next with Niall, we can sit together at the front.'

Mrs Oliver sighed.

'She can go in front of me,' I said.

Copyright © Naomi Richards and Julia Hague 2016

I wasn't sure why I'd said it. But there was something about the look on Mrs Oliver's face that had made me offer.

'Oh Niall, how kind,' Mrs Oliver said and smiled gratefully.

Liam glared at me.

Liam, Justin and I were good friends. Sitting together would have been great.

I sat down behind Lexi. Liam turned around to give me another glare. I shrugged.

The seat was still a good view and I could watch the pantomime in peace – no distraction from my friends.

At the interval Lexi turned around and said 'thank you' to me for letting her have a front row seat.

She said she wasn't sure why Mrs Oliver wanted her to sit there but it was a lovely surprise anyway.

I felt secretly happy that I wasn't sitting with Liam and Justin because they kept on getting told to be quiet. I hated getting told off.

I bet you're thinking that's the reason I was glad I gave my seat up.

Well it wasn't.

When the pantomime finished the actors all took bows and we all stood up and cheered and clapped.

Then one of the actors asked us to sit down again.

He explained that today was not only a special day for the pantomime because it was their last show before Christmas, but it was also a special day for someone else.

Then he walked to the front of the stage and asked if there was someone called Lexi in the audience.

He had heard she was sitting in the front row.

Lexi put her hand up slowly. I could see her cheeks were going bright red even though I was sitting behind her.

The actor asked her to come up on the stage.

Everyone clapped.

Then Mrs Oliver moved across and gestured for Lexi to go up on the stage and took her hand and led her up the steps at the front.

Then it happened.

This wonderful thing.

Copyright © Naomi Richards and Julia Hague 2016

The reason why I was so happy that she had my seat on the front row.

Out from behind the curtains, which were behind the actor, walked a man in uniform.

I watched as Lexi squealed and then ran across the stage and jumped into his arms.

It was her dad.

Her dad was a soldier and he was home for Christmas to be with his family.

Lexi's mother had arranged for the surprise with the theatre and the school.

And Lexi had to be on the front row.

So they could ask for her to come up on the stage easily.

Mrs Oliver thanked me again after the show.

But she didn't need to.

I learned something special that day.

Sometimes you don't know why you put someone before you.

Sometimes you might not ever find out.

But when you do, and it's something as great as seeing someone's dad come home for Christmas, it's the nicest feeling in the world.

Copyright © Naomi Richards and Julia Hague 2016

NOTES TO SUPPORT THE DISCUSSION

Niall did not ask any questions when he heard that someone else needed a front seat in the theatre. He just offered his own. Once he realized why the front seat was needed he felt good that he had made the girl in the class happy. He learnt a valuable lesson that day – if you are asked to help someone or give up something, say you will and believe that there is a valid reason why. There will always be a good enough reason, even if you don't know at the beginning.

DISCUSSION QUESTIONS TO ASK THE CHILDREN

- How did the story make you feel?

- What did Niall learn that day?

- Would you have done the same as Niall?

- Do you think Niall's friends learnt anything?

- How would you have felt if you were Lexi?

- What do you think she felt about getting Niall's seat?

- What does it mean to you to be kind?

ACTIVITIES TO DO WITH THE CHILDREN

THOUGHTS
Ask the children to write a story about a child who was not kind but then something happened and he/she changed.

GETTING POETIC
Get the children to write a poem about being kind and how it makes them feel.

SCHOOL MOTTO
What motto can the children come up with in groups of four to promote kindness at school? Ask them to design a shield and put their motto on it.

THANK YOU

In twos, get the children to consider the ways we can say thank you to someone who has done something kind for us. Ask them to list them on a piece of paper and then share them with the group.

FIGURING IT OUT

(ABOUT BEING DYSCALCULIC)

JACK'S STORY

EDUCATORS' NOTES

Suggested age for story – 8–10 years old

Children are very aware of other children's achievements and what they are able to do. They know which of their friends are good at spelling, reading or maths and they know which of their friends are not as good.

Children also talk about the books they are reading and the scores they get in their lessons and don't really think about how it can make others feel. They need to be sensitive to all the children in their class and their abilities.

It is apparent to a child who has difficulty with a subject or subjects, or perhaps has a special need or learning difficulty, that they may not be as bright as the others and they may need a little extra help to do as well.

This story teaches children that we are not all the same and that it is okay to get extra help. When a child has this help and starts to thrive they gain confidence in their schoolwork and this can improve their mood, meaning happier friendships, better work and achieving more.

All pre- and post-lesson exercises can be used for evaluation purposes if required.

LEARNING OUTCOMES

- It is okay to have extra help in lessons.

- If you find work hard it is better to ask for help than struggle alone.

- Everyone has something that they find hard to do.

- We need to be kind to those who aren't as able in some subjects as we are.

INTRODUCTION STATEMENT

We cannot all be good at everything and not everyone finds everything easy. Yes, of course, we have to practise to get better at something. Well, most of us do. But what do you do when you keep on practising in the hope of getting better but you don't? This may happen to you because your brain works in a different way to other people's. There is nothing wrong with that. If it does work differently then you may need to find a different way to learn something. Some people learn by drawing pictures, some with words and some through acting it out or repeating parrot fashion.

You have to find the right learning style for you if you find something more challenging. If you're feeling miserable or frustrated when you're trying to get something right, it's better to tell someone than let it continue. They can then help you find the right way for you to learn.

PRE- AND POST-LESSON EXERCISE
Before reading the story ask the children to write down what they think about children who have a teaching assistant or a helper in the class. After the story, ask them again to write down what they think.

This story is all about a child who found numbers difficult and how he got help once someone realized what the problem was. Let's meet Jack.

JACK'S STORY

For most kids, learning your times tables is something you do, get your gold star on the chart in the classroom for and then move on to the next thing. It's a part of school life.

For most kids, multiplication and division and numbers can be fun.

For most kids.

I'm not most kids.

I'm different.

Sure, I always think I can learn my times tables. I spend all night chanting one of them over and over to get them in my head.

Then I go to bed. Get up. Go to school.

Gone.

I can't remember what I've learnt.

I concentrate and concentrate.

I squeeze my face tight like squeezing it harder will make the numbers pop out suddenly.

Nothing.

Maybe one of them or two of them if I'm lucky. The rest disappear.

So just when the class is going on to the next times table, I'm still struggling with the first. And so it goes on.

See I'm dyscalculic.

One fancy word for one simple thing. I can't do numbers.

At first, when no one knew I had it, I used to sit in my bedroom doing maths homework and kick the desk.

In front of me was my exercise book and the maths book.

No matter how much I tried to get the numbers to add up or whatever it was I was supposed to be doing with them, they wouldn't.

I hated numbers.

So I kicked the desk.

Hard.

When Mum or Dad used to try and help me with the homework I would get angry and shout and say I didn't want to do it.

Copyright © Naomi Richards and Julia Hague 2016

At first everyone thought I was just being lazy.

Not wanting to work or something.

But then, after a bit, they realized it was only happening with maths.

I was near the top of the class in English and getting on fine with everything else.

Unless numbers were involved.

Mum told me I got so angry because I was frustrated with not being able to do what others were doing.

Then my teacher realized that I wasn't seeing the numbers the same as other people saw them.

That my times tables were a mountain to climb and not a small hill like the rest of the class.

So I got help.

A nice teacher comes in to see me twice a week at school and goes over the maths the class are doing.

I no longer have to kick the desk at home, because I'm not frustrated.

And I'm not scared of numbers anymore.

I don't like them much.

I like letters more. And spelling and stuff.

But I'm not scared.

Maybe my times tables will always be a struggle.

Maybe numbers will always be something difficult for me.

My nice teacher has told me that I might find foreign languages difficult too. But he also told me that understanding that I need help and getting it is always the solution.

That there are a lot of subjects at school that maths isn't a part of.

That he can help me get to a level where I can just cope with maths rather than be good at it.

And I know now that being different doesn't matter.

That when you look at everyone else, they're all different.

Finding numbers hard or letters hard or not being able to paint well or act well or do sport are all okay.

I wish I'd told Mum and Dad right at the start, when I was very little, when I felt scared that I couldn't understand numbers.

Copyright © Naomi Richards and Julia Hague 2016

Then I might have got the nice teacher earlier.
And I wouldn't have kicked my desk in my bedroom.
I'm not scared of numbers anymore.
And that's brilliant.

Copyright © Naomi Richards and Julia Hague 2016

NOTES TO SUPPORT THE DISCUSSION

Jack was much happier when he got the help he needed in the classroom. Before that it must have been very frustrating for him and his mum and dad because he could not remember his times tables.

Finding out and giving a name to your 'struggle' is a good thing because then you can find the best way of learning for you. There are so many children who need a bit of help that it has become normal.

DISCUSSION QUESTIONS TO ASK THE CHILDREN

- What do you think about Jack?

- How did he handle finding out he was dyscalculic and having a teacher help him?

- How do you think he felt?

- Is there anything you feel you struggle with?

- Who would you talk to if you found something hard?

- How would you help someone who was dyscalculic?

ACTIVITIES TO DO WITH THE CHILDREN

GIVING ADVICE

What would the children say to a friend if they found something difficult? Get them to discuss the difficulty with a friend in the group.

NUMBERS AND WORDS

Get the children into groups and ask them to create a word search that is made up of numbers or words. They have to add in ten words or ten number sequences that the educator provides. Once completed the teacher should hand them out to other members of the group for them to complete.

RESEARCH

Get the children to research on the internet one of the following learning difficulties children have and write five bullet points about it: dyscalculia, dyslexia, dysgraphia or dyspraxia.

CELEBRITY CHALLENGE

Ask the children to find the name of a celebrity who finds numbers, words or language difficult and stick all the names up on the whiteboard.